D0872074

HARVARD HISTORICAL MONOGRAPHS
XLIII

Published under the direction of the Department of History
from the income of The Robert Louis Stroock Fund

Ottoman Imperialism
and
German Protestantism

1521-1555

STEPHEN A. FISCHER-GALATI

OCTAGON BOOKS

A DIVISION OF FARRAR, STRAUS AND GIROUX

New York 1972

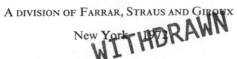

Reprinted 1972
by special arrangement with Harvard University Press

OCTAGON BOOKS
A Division of Farrar, Straus & Giroux, Inc.
19 Union Square West
New York, N. Y. 10003

Library of Congress Catalog Card Number: 71-159184

ISBN 0-374-92747-2

Printed in U.S.A. by
NOBLE OFFSET PRINTERS, INC.
NEW YORK 3, N. Y.

To the Memory of Robert Pierpont Blake

Preface

The effect of the conflict between Hapsburg and Turk on the course
of the Reformation has been discussed by various historians since
Ranke, but to a very limited extent and chiefly in terms of German
history. In the absence of a comprehensive and systematic study
the character and significance of the relation has remained obscure.
I undertook such a task after making a critical examination of the
available German literature and investigation of various unexplored
sources on relevant aspects of Ottoman, Hapsburg, and German
history. My ultimate goal was to determine the nature and extent
of the Turkish impact on the German Reformation in the crucial
years before the Religious Peace of Augsburg, within the broader
framework of East-West relations in the sixteenth century. Preliminary findings and conclusions were incorporated in my doctoral
dissertation, "The Turkish Impact on the German Reformation,
1520–1555," completed in 1949. Careful reinvestigation of the problem and revision of the original manuscript has resulted in the
present monograph.

For the continuous encouragement of Professor Myron P. Gil-
more, who introduced me to the study of early modern European
history, and the late Professor Robert P. Blake whose enthusiasm
and erudition stimulated my own interest in Ottoman problems,
I am deeply grateful. I am also indebted to Professor Halil Inalcik,
of the University of Ankara, for much relevant information based
on his work in sixteenth-century Turkish history, to Professors
Margaret Sterne, of Wayne State University, and Wallace T. Mac-
Caffrey, of Haverford College, for many valuable suggestions and
to my wife, Anne D'Esterre, for painstaking editorial efforts and
general criticism. Grateful acknowledgement is also made to the
publishers of *Church History, Archiv für Reformationsgeschichte,*
and *Südost-Forschungen* for permission to reprint passages from

my articles cited in the bibliography. Research grants from the American Philosophical Society and Wayne State University made possible the final revision of the manuscript.

Stephen A. Fischer-Galati

Wayne State University
Detroit, Michigan

Contents

I. The Legacy of Maximilian I   1

II. The Turks and the Protestants   13

III. The Price of Protestant Aid   38

IV. Hapsburg Policy between Turk and Protestants   57

V. The Results of Hapsburg Policy   97

VI. Conclusion   111

Bibliography   121

Index   137

Ottoman Imperialism
and
German Protestantism
1521-1555

Chapter I

The Legacy of Maximilian I

The second half of the fifteenth century was a period of drastic change in the political and social configuration of southeastern Europe. The Ottoman Turks, who had been threatening the Balkan Peninsula since their first appearance as an organized power in the early years of the fourteenth century, had at last achieved the conquest of Constantinople, long one of the main goals of their European policy. The fall of the Byzantine capital on May 29, 1453, did not mark the beginning of a new era in the Balkans; it was, however, the successful culmination of the efforts of the Osmanlis to establish themselves there as the leading power.

Before 1453 the armies of the Turkish sultans had conquered only Bulgaria and a substantial part of the Greek peninsula. Serbia, overrun in 1389, had not been incorporated into the Ottoman Empire; Wallachia, though tributary since 1417, still maintained its own social and political organization; Moldavia, Hungary, and the Hapsburg possessions of Styria, Carinthia, and Carniola, although occasionally subjected to attack, were in no immediate danger of invasion. With the conquest of Constantinople and the subsequent replacement of the decadent Byzantine Empire by a strong and efficient political organization, the outlook for Western Europe changed considerably. Within less than a decade the armies of Mohammed the Conqueror had subdued Serbia, Greece, and Wallachia, thus consolidating, geographically at least, their holdings in the Balkan Peninsula. At the same time, to protect these possessions, Turkish forces engaged in relentless raids into the territories of the Kingdom of Hungary, their most powerful neighbor and once the leading contender for supremacy in southeastern Europe.[1]

During the rule of the powerful Anjou dynasty, especially under Louis the Great (1342–1382), Hungary had occupied a leading position in Eastern Europe. Bulgaria, Croatia, and the Danubian principalities were virtually puppets of the Angevin state. Only Stephen Dushan with his dreams of an eastern Serbian Empire constituted an obstacle to Hungarian domination of the Balkans. But Hungarian supremacy was short-lived. Undermined by the opposition of a Greek Orthodox population to a Roman Catholic master, it was further jeopardized by the Turkish incursions into Serbia, Bulgaria, and Wallachia. Even the weak successors of Louis the Great understood that the capture of Sofia and Tirnovo, the disaster of Kosovo, and the lost battle of Rovine heralded the end of Hungarian ascendancy in the Balkan Peninsula.

With Magyar influence declining and further Turkish attacks imminent, King Sigismund (1387–1437) tried to rally Western Christendom against the "enemy of the faith." His efforts were only partially successful. The Western rulers, concerned with their own problems, refused to undertake concerted action against the advancing Turk. Nevertheless, several Western knights and adventurers, allied with a few Balkan princes, joined Sigismund in the crusade which ended in the catastrophe of Nicopolis in 1396.

Nicopolis might have proved fatal to Hungary, had it not been for the unexpected relief resulting from the Turkish rout at Angora in 1402. Crushed by Tamerlane, it took the Ottoman Turks nearly twenty years to regain their strength. But the Hungarians did not take advantage of this unequaled opportunity to reestablish their position in the Balkans. Sigismund pursued a policy of dynastic expansion in Central Europe, while the magnates strove to strengthen their local authority at the expense of the absent king, the unruly towns, and the lesser nobility. Only in the twenties, when

---

[1] On the European conquests of the Ottoman Turks see J. von Hammer, *Histoire de l'Empire Ottoman* (J. J. Hellert, tr., Paris, 1836), I, 162 ff., II, 1 ff.; N. Jorga, *Geschichte des Osmanischen Reiches* (Gotha, 1908), I, 147 ff., II, 3 ff.; J. W. Zinkeisen, *Geschichte des Osmanischen Reiches in Europa* (Gotha, 1840), I, 184 ff., II, 3 ff.

the Turks under Murad II renewed their offensive, did the Magyars belatedly awaken to their danger. In spite of their victory over the Osmanlis in 1443, the Hungarians' predominance in the Balkan Peninsula was ended. In fact, by the middle of the fifteenth century their main concern was to defend their own country against the attacks of the Ottomans.[2]

Fortunately for Hungary, however, the Turks, upon completing the conquest of the Balkan Peninsula, made no further attempt at territorial expansion into Eastern Europe. Apparently satisfied with the extent of his empire in the West, Mohammed II turned his attention toward the Mediterranean and the work of internal consolidation of the Ottoman state. While the Turks were warring with Venice and profound transformations were taking place in the social, political, and economic structure of the Balkan countries, the King of Hungary, Matthias Corvinus, attempted to expand the frontiers of his kingdom at the expense of the weak Frederick III of Hapsburg.[3]

Frederick III, Holy Roman Emperor and custodian of his family's possessions in Eastern Europe, was a failure in both roles. Less interested in affairs of state than in collecting jewels and dabbling in the occult, he was unable to check anarchy within the Empire or to prevent the loss of Bohemia to George Poděbrad and Hungary to Matthias Corvinus. Such a man, whose only positive achievements were the conclusion of a marriage between his son Maximilian and Mary of Burgundy and the devising of the motto *Austriae est imperare omni universo,* was easy prey for the ambitious Hungarian monarch.[4]

From his accession in 1458 Corvinus pursued a determined policy

[2] On the rise and decline of Hungarian power in the Balkan Peninsula consult D. G. Kosary, *A History of Hungary* (Cleveland, 1941), 44 ff.; L. Kupelwieser, *Die Kämpfe Ungarns mit den Osmanen bis zur Schlacht bei Mohács, 1526* (Wien, 1899), 3 ff.; O. Zarek, *The History of Hungary* (London, 1939), 147 ff., as well as the references under note 1.

[3] The best monograph on Matthias Corvinus is by W. Fraknói, *Matthias Corvinus, König von Ungarn, 1458–1490* (Freiburg im Breisgau, 1891).

[4] The best study of the reign of Frederick III is by V. von Kraus, *Deutsche Geschichte zur Zeit Albrechts II und Friedrichs III. 1438–1486* (Stuttgart, 1905), 55 ff.

of territorial aggrandizement. Instead of provoking the Turks by a southward expansion, the Hungarian, first reinforced his frontiers against possible Ottoman incursions, then turned westward against Frederick. In 1463 he administered a preliminary defeat to the weak Emperor, who had been scheming with a group of magnates to overthrow Corvinus and reestablish Hapsburg rule in Hungary. Following a period of temporary peace, during which Matthias failed in an attempt to annex Bohemia and was obliged to defend himself against the King of Poland, he attacked Frederick again. In 1485, taking advantage of a rebellion of the Austrian nobility, Matthias Corvinus invaded and conquered most of Austria, including Vienna, thus partly realizing his plan for expansion into Central Europe. But his success was transient, for after his death in 1490 the power of Hungary declined rapidly, while Maximilian I, Holy Roman Emperor since 1493, was laying the foundations for Hapsburg supremacy.[5]

Hapsburg aspirations in Central and Eastern Europe can be traced back as far as 1273, when Rudolph I was elected Holy Roman Emperor, but it was not until the beginning of the reign of Maximilian I that a policy of conquest was clearly formulated. Prior to 1491, even though the Hapsburgs possessed, or had dynastic claims to, Austria, the Tyrol, Bohemia, Hungary, Styria, Carinthia, Carniola, and, since 1477, Burgundy, these territories were not under the direct control of any single individual, but divided among the various branches of the family. Only with the death of Ladislas the Posthumus in 1457, the renunciation of the Tyrol by Sigismund in 1490, and the conclusion of the Treaty of Pressburg of 1491, did all the claims and possessions fall into the hands of one man, Emperor Maximilian I.[6]

[5] For Matthias Corvinus' foreign policy consult Fraknói, *Matthias Corvinus,* 57 ff.; Kupelwieser, *Kämpfe Ungarns,* 136 ff. On Maximilian I see K. Kaser, *Deutsche Geschichte zur Zeit Maximilians I* (Stuttgart, 1912); R. W. Seton-Watson, *Maximilian I* (Westminster, 1902); H. Ulmann, *Kaiser Maximilian I* (Stuttgart, 1884), vols. I, II.

[6] The complex dynastic problems connected with the history of the House of Hapsburg are ably discussed by G. Turba, *Geschichte des Thronfolgerechts in allen habsburgischen Ländern bis zur pragmatischen Sanktion Kaiser Karls VI* (Wien, 1903), 7 ff.

Maximilian had been the virtual head of the House of Hapsburg and of the Holy Roman Empire since his election as King of the Romans in 1486. A dedicated exponent of the device, *Austriae est imperare omni universo,* he explored every opportunity to enhance the position of his family. In the west, as husband of Mary of Burgundy, he sought to strengthen the Burgundian Duchy against the continuous interference of the French king, Louis XI. In the south, Maximilian renewed the imperial claims to Italy and even contemplated the conquest of Venice in an effort to gain access to the Mediterranean. In the east, the Emperor's aims were to be elected King of Hungary, to regain the Kingdom of Bohemia, to arrest the advance of the Ottoman Turks toward the Hapsburg possessions, and perhaps even expand the boundaries of the Holy Roman Empire as far as Constantinople. Although he made serious efforts to realize his ambitions in Western and Southern Europe, his main achievements were those connected with his Eastern policy.[7]

In 1490, the Hungarian magnates, mindful of the late Matthias Corvinus' attempts to limit their power, decided to elect a nonentity as his successor. Disregarding the possibility of a Turkish offensive and their treaty obligations toward the Hapsburgs, they chose as their ruler the feeble Ladislas of Bohemia. The selfish policy of the Hungarian nobility was to bring severe consequences. Although they were correct in minimizing the danger from Bayazid II, who was more concerned with domestic affairs than with westward expansion, ignoring Maximilian's claims to the Hungarian throne was a dangerous error.

In 1463, upon the conclusion of the first war between Frederick and Corvinus, the Emperor had been able to obtain the promise that his son Maximilian would succeed Corvinus as king. Frederick apparently did not attach much importance to this understanding,

---

[7] The problems of Maximilian's foreign policy are ably discussed by A. Dopsch, "Die Weltstaatpolitik der Habsburger im Werden ihres Grossreiches (1477–1526)," *Gesamtdeutsche Vergangenheit. Festgabe für Heinrich Ritter von Srbik zum 60. Geburtstag am 10. November 1938* (München, 1938), 55–62; K. Kaser, "Die auswärtige Politik Maximilians I," *Mitteilungen des Instituts für österreichische Geschichtsforschung,* XXVI (1905), 612–626; Kaser, *Deutsche Geschichte,* 17 ff.

as he did not expect the Hungarians to abide by it. Maximilian, however, did not wish to be deprived of his rights. Realizing that victory over Ladislas would bring him both the Hungarian and the Bohemian crowns, he took up arms. But, although he forced the Hungarians to evacuate Austria, he was not strong enough to overthrow Ladislas altogether. By the Treaty of Pressburg, Maximilian had to be content with the promise that he would succeed his rival in Hungary and Bohemia should there be no direct heirs. Apparently satisfied with these terms, Maximilian (seemingly, little concerned over the possibility of a Turkish attack against Hungary or the eastern possessions of the Hapsburgs) turned southward and engaged in the Italian wars ignited by Charles VIII's invasion of 1494. Here he met with even less success. Enmeshed by the skillful diplomacy and maneuvers of the Papacy, Venice, Charles of France, and Ferdinand of Spain, the Emperor suffered a series of diplomatic and military setbacks. He decided in 1501 to withdraw from Italy and pursue a policy which he expected would meet with the approval of the inhabitants of the Empire.[8]

One of the main reasons for Maximilian's failure in Italy was financial embarrassment. His own resources, derived chiefly from Austria, were insufficient for large-scale operations and had to be supplemented with funds granted by the imperial Diets. The Diets of the late fifteenth and early sixteenth centuries, however, did not wish to support Maximilian's Italian venture, as their own problems appeared far more pressing.

The political anarchy prevalent in Germany throughout the fifteenth century reached its height during the later years of Frederick's life. The Emperor was a figurehead, and the central government virtually nonexistent. The oppressed and restless masses were ruled by a large number of almost autonomous princes and free cities desirous of political and economic advantages at the expense of the imperial power and weaker neighbors. The infrequent Diets accomplished nothing for the welfare of the Empire, as the members were absorbed in quarrels over legal recognition of usurped

[8] Maximilian's Italian policy is well treated by Ulmann, *Kaiser Maximilian I*, I, 40 ff., II, 359 ff.; Kaser, *Deutsche Geschichte*, 45 ff., 110 ff.

privileges and positions. By the end of Frederick's reign the situation had become so serious that some of the leading German princes were perturbed. Headed by Berthold of Henneberg, Elector of Mainz, a small group of magnates organized a movement to reform the imperial administration. But their ideas involved so drastic a curtailment of the prerogatives and powers of the emperor that they were strenuously opposed even by the irresolute Frederick III. Besides, the majority of the princes and cities, while agreeing to the need for reform, continued to encourage anarchy in Germany. These incredibly bad political conditions, aggravated by occasional peasant risings, were part of Maximilian's inheritance.[9]

The new emperor considered domestic affairs subordinate to foreign policy. As he regarded Germany primarily as a source of revenue for the execution of his dynastic ambitions, he did not hesitate to promise the reformers concessions in return for subsidies for his Italian wars. The princes and cities were extremely responsive to the Emperor's willingness to call the Diets periodically, trusting that in return for meager subsidies they could gain substantial advantages at his expense. However, no compromise could be reached between the opposing parties. The Diets insisted on reforms prior to grants of subsidies; whereas Maximilian, who did not wish his power curtailed, insisted on subsidies before reforms. Under such conditions little could be accomplished. Only on two occasions, at Worms in 1495 and at Augsburg in 1500, were the opponents able to reach an understanding; but, as neither side expected the other to keep its promises, the Emperor received very few subsidies and the reformers very few concessions.[10]

---

[9] On German internal conditions and the "Reform Movement" see H. Baron, "Imperial Reform and the Hapsburgs, 1486–1504," *The American Historical Review*, XLIV (1938–39), 293–303; Kaser, *Deutsche Geschichte*, 171 ff.; J. Janssen, *History of the German People at the Close of the Middle Ages* (M. A. Mitchell and A. M. Christie, tr., London, 1896), I, 307 ff., II, 1 ff., 161 ff., 206 ff.; L. von Ranke, *History of the Reformation in Germany* (S. Austin, tr., London, 1845), I, 51 ff.; von Kraus, *Deutsche Geschichte*, 55 ff.

[10] On Maximilian's struggles with the Diets see A. Kluckhohn *et al.*, ed., *Deutsche Reichstagsakten unter Kaiser Karl V* (Gotha, 1893–   ), I, 3 ff.

As a result, the Emperor decided to alter his foreign policy. In the early years of the sixteenth century the King of Hungary seemed anxious to conclude a marriage alliance with the Hapsburgs, and there had been some agitation in Germany for a crusade against the Turks. Maximilian believed that a reorientation of his policy toward the East might not only prove advantageous to himself, but would also meet with the approval of the Diets. Therefore, when in 1502 Ladislas suggested the possibility of a dynastic alliance between the Jagellons and the Hapsburgs, Maximilian responded with alacrity to his overtures. Already successful in negotiating the extraordinary marriage between his son Philip and Joanna of Spain, as well as his own less impressive one to Bianca Sforza, the Emperor welcomed the opportunity to arrange another important union which would insure the consolidation of his family's position in Eastern Europe. In 1506, despite the opposition of the Hungarian magnates who expected their leader, John Zápolya, to succeed Ladislas, Maximilian was able to bring about a double betrothal between his granddaughter Mary and Ladislas' infant son Louis, and one of his grandsons, Charles or Ferdinand, to Louis' sister Anna. It took Maximilian ten years to subdue the opposition of Zápolya and his party, but in 1515, by the Treaty of Vienna, he gained ratification of the arrangements of 1506. Through diplomatic means, Maximilian had assured his family the succession in Hungary and Bohemia.[11] He was to be less successful in attaining the other goal of his eastern policy, a crusade against the Ottoman Turks.

_____

(to be subsequently referred to as DRA); J. J. Müller, ed., *Des Heiligen Römischen Reichs Teutscher Nation Reichstagsstaat von Anno 1500 bis 1509 unter Kaysers Maximiliani I Regierung* (Jena, 1709); J. J. Müller, ed., *Des Heil Römischen Reichs Teutscher Nation Reichs Tags Theatrum wie selbigis unter Keyser Maximilian I* (Jena, 1718), vols. I, II; J. J. Schmauss, ed., *Neue und vollständigere Sammlung der Reichsabschiede welche von den Zeiten Kayser Conrads des II bis Jetzo auf den Teutschen Reichs-Tägen abgefasset worden* (Franckfurt am Mayn, 1747), I², 33 ff.

[11] Maximilian's Hungarian policy is ably discussed in X. Liske, "Der Congress zu Wien im Jahre 1515," *Forschungen zur deutschen Geschichte*, VII (Göttingen, 1867), 463–558; Kaser, *Deutsche Geschichte*, 40 ff., 156 ff.; Ulmann, *Kaiser Maximilian I*, II, 538 ff.

Maximilian's eagerness to fight the Turks is best explained in terms of his dynastic policy. Although he did cherish the hope of resuscitating the Byzantine state and becoming basileus of a Byzantino-Hapsburg empire, his actual desire for war was prompted by more immediate and realistic concerns. The sultans of the late fifteenth and early sixteenth centuries, Bayazid II and Selim I, while not primarily interested in westward expansion, nevertheless made intermittent raids into southern Hungary and the Hapsburg possessions of Styria, Carinthia, and Carniola. These activities were resented by Maximilian who, after 1506, became increasingly anxious to protect the interests of his family in the East. Moreover, since Bayazid and Selim spent most of their reign either in Constantinople or fighting in the Middle East, the Emperor thought of exploiting this situation to strengthen Eastern Europe against the eventual renewal of the Turkish offensive, and perhaps gain some territory at the expense of the Ottoman Empire.[12]

These plans, however, could not be executed without the help of dependable allies, as the Turks were a much more formidable adversary than the mercenaries of the Venetians or the French. Failing to obtain support from the West, Maximilian turned once more to the Diets, although he was aware of their reluctance to subsidize his foreign enterprises. He was not altogether unjustified in asking their assistance, as some of the Germans at least seemed interested in undertaking a crusade against the "enemy of the faith."

The fifteenth-century Germans, like their western neighbors were in general unperturbed by the fall of Constantinople and subsequent enslavement of the Balkan Peninsula by the Turks. Except for a few scattered pamphlets condemning the conquerors for their religion rather than their aggressions, the Germans did not express disapproval of the changes occuring in southeastern Europe; nor did they advocate any action against the Infidel. The

[12] For Maximilian's plans against the Turks consult E. Charrière, ed., *Négociations de la France dans le Levant* (Paris, 1848), I, 49–63; J. Ursu, *La Politique Orientale de François I, 1515–1547* (Paris, 1908), 7 ff.; Ulmann, *Kaiser Maximilian I*, I, 204 ff., II, 555 ff.; J. W. Zinkeisen, ed., *Drei Denkschriften über die orientalische Frage von Papst Leo X, König Franz I von Frankreich und Kaiser Maximilian I aus dem Jahre 1517* (Gotha, 1854), 63 ff.

attempts of Nicholas V, Calixtus III, and Pius II to instigate a crusade were completely unsuccessful. By the end of the century, however, the intellectuals became quite vociferous in their demands for action against the Turks. These men, chiefly the followers of the new humanism, seemed convinced that the greatness of the German nation could be restored through a successful crusade led by the Holy Roman Emperor. Throughout Maximilian's reign, men like Brant, Hutten, Wimphelling, Gengenback, Locher, and many others, clamored in speeches and writings for immediate action.

Maximilian hoped that the humanists might influence the Diets to grant him subsidies for the execution of his anti-Turkish schemes. In fact, he exaggerated the seriousness of the threat to the Empire in order to arouse the *Reichstag*. Unfortunately for his plans, neither the writings of his admirers nor his own speeches at the Diets could persuade the princes and cities that military action against a remote enemy was of greater importance than their own problems, the *Bundschuh* revolts, or, after 1517, the appearance of Luther. In Diet after Diet, the same princes and the representatives of the same cities gave Maximilian the same answer: no support for ventures outside the Empire. Clearly, the members of the *Reichstage,* and for that matter the apathetic masses too, did not agree with Maximilian and his supporters that a strong Turkish policy was essential for the welfare of the Empire and the Hapsburgs. Under the circumstances, the Emperor's eastern ambitions could not be realized, and he had to be content with the gains made in Hungary and Bohemia.[13]

---

[13] For general considerations on the Turkish question and German public opinion consult L. Gerstenberg, *Zur Geschichte des deutschen Türkenschauspiels* (Meppen, 1902), 15 ff.; B. Kamil, *Die Türken in der deutschen Literatur bis zum Barock und die Sultangestalten in den Türkendramen Lowensteins* (Kiel, 1935), 5 ff.; A. Scholtze, *Die orientalische Frage in der öffentlichen Meinung des sechszehnten Jahrhunderts* (Frankenberg, 1880), 3 ff.; R. Wolkan, "Zu den Türkenliedern des XVI. Jahrhunderts," *Festschrift zum VIII. allgemeinen deutschen Neuphilologentage in Wien* (Wien, 1898), 65 ff. See also R. von Liliencron, *Die historischen Volkslieder der Deutschen vom 13 bis 16 Jahrhundert* (Leipzig, 1865), II, 312 ff., III, 28 ff., 41 ff., 67 ff., 100 ff., 212 ff.

During the last few years of his reign, Maximilian was unable to advance the cause of the House of Hapsburg in Europe. Forced to abandon his Turkish projects by the opposition of the Diets, he also had to renounce his Italian plans because of French opposition and his usual lack of funds. In 1516 he withdrew from the Italian wars (which he had reentered in 1508), having fulfilled none of his goals there. However, Maximilian did not need to be ashamed of the legacy which he was to leave his successor.

In his lifetime he had succeeded in consolidating the Burgundian inheritance; he had paved the way for a policy of intervention in Italy by reviving the imperial idea and contracting the Sforza marriage; he had assured the Hapsburg succession and control in Hungary and Bohemia. Before his death in 1519 he had the satisfaction of seeing Charles, his successor as Holy Roman Emperor, become King of Aragon and Castile. Truly, Maximilian had laid the foundation of Hapsburg glory in Europe. The inheritance of his grandson was, however, more impressive in appearance than in reality. The Holy Roman Empire, to which Charles succeeded in 1519, was in a state of chaos, the Lutheran revolt having aggravated the tension and anarchy which had prevailed throughout most of Maximilian's reign. In Italy conditions were not much better. Despite a temporary truce between the contending powers, the situation was just as confused in 1519 as it had been twenty years earlier. Nor was the outlook more encouraging in Hungary. The magnates, though at peace with the Hapsburgs, had not forgotten their hatred for the foreign intruder. They occupied themselves in extirpating the resistance of the oppressed peasantry (which had revolted in 1514), while pursuing their usual policy of extracting concessions from the weak Ladislas. The expectation of a resumption of the Turkish offensive was a further complicating factor. Indeed, within three years of Maximilian's death, Suleiman the Magnificent was to renew the onslaught against Central Europe.

The burden of the legacy was, however, not equally borne by Charles and Ferdinand. The former, who had inherited the German and Italian problems, was in a better position to cope with the situation than his younger brother. Already ruler of Burgundy and Spain, the Emperor commanded enough funds to carry out the imperial policy in Italy without the assistance of the German Diets. Moreover, as he had been trained in the art of government from an early age, he was surrounded by advisers and executives, including Ferdinand, who could attend to the affairs of Germany while he himself was trying to gain control over the Italian peninsula.[14] Ferdinand's case was very different. The younger Hapsburg, who had inherited Austria and had acquired through his marriage to Anna of Hungary the responsibility of promoting and defending his family's interests in the East, had neither the ability nor the means to handle the extremely complex Hungarian situation. Lacking political experience and imagination, he was unable to combat the activities of the nobility; without sufficient personal resources, he had to rely on his brother and the German Diets to save Hungary from invasion by the Turk and to defend his interests in Eastern Europe after the disaster of Mohacs. Nor was he able to fill adequately his position as *Staathalter* in Germany, assumed upon Charles' departure for Italy in 1521. To check the spread of the Reformation would have been a difficult task for the most skilled statesman; it proved far beyond the capacity of the young and essentially powerless Ferdinand.[15]

Under these trying circumstances, Ferdinand, *Staathalter* and guardian of the Hapsburg interests in the East, often mishandled the complex German and Hungarian situations. His actions, together with those of Charles, Holy Roman Emperor and custodian of the Hapsburg interests in the West, were to have grave repercussions. Maximilian's legacy, in its negative aspects, was to play a decisive part during the next few decades in shaping the course of the history of Hungary, Germany, and the German Reformation.

[14] The history of Charles' early years is admirably covered by K. Brandi, *Kaiser Karl V* (München, 1937), 19 ff.

[15] For the history of Ferdinand's early years see W. Bauer, *Die Anfänge Ferdinands I* (Wien, 1907). For his Eastern policy consult L. Kupelwieser, *Die Kämpfe Oesterreichs mit den Osmanen vom Jahre 1526 bis 1537* (Wien, 1899), 1 ff.; Kupelwieser, *Die Kämpfe Ungarns*, 186 ff.

Chapter II

The Turks and the Protestants

The accession of Suleiman I to the throne of the Ottoman Empire brought about a reorientation of Turkish foreign policy. The new sultan, satisfied with the results of his father's victorious campaigns in Egypt and Persia, resumed the onslaught against southeastern Europe. Belgrade, the key fortress on the Danube that had withstood Turkish assaults for over half a century, finally collapsed in 1521; the road to Hungary was opened. The fall of Rhodes, the main Christian stronghold in the eastern Mediterranean, in 1522 further darkened the outlook for Eastern Europe.[1]

The renewal of the Turkish offensive in Europe had alarmed the Mediterranean world and Hungary. Venice, as usual, took urgent measures to insinuate herself into the sultan's good graces. In return for various concessions she obtained a favorable commercial treaty from the Porte in 1521. Pope Adrian VI, disturbed by the siege of Rhodes and fearing a repetition of Otranto should the Knights of Saint John fail to hold back the Infidel, beseeched Francis I, Henry VIII, and Charles V to save the island. He recommended a general crusade as the best solution. But the quarrelsome Christian monarchs questioned Adrian's motives and the gravity of the Turkish threat. Thus the fate of Rhodes was sealed.[2]

The fall of Belgrade and Rhodes increased the pressure on Hun-

[1] On Suleiman and the effect of his accession on European society see von Hammer, *Histoire*, V, 1 ff.; Jorga, *Geschichte*, II, 342 ff.; R. B. Merriman, *Suleiman the Magnificent, 1520–1566* (Cambridge, 1944), 31 ff.; Zinkeisen, *Geschichte des Osmanischen Reiches*, II, 611 ff.

[2] On Adrian's attitude see L. P. Gachard, ed., *Correspondance de Charles-Quint et d'Adrien VI* (Brussels, 1859), 1 ff.

gary. Louis' kingdom was not prepared to resist a major Turkish offensive. The king was weak, the nobility restless, the peasantry rebellious. The country was recovering but slowly from the devastation caused by the Peasant Revolt of 1514.[3] Thus beset, Louis could think of no better allies than his powerful Hapsburg neighbors; not only did they share common political interests but they were also closely related by marriage.[4] But hopes of succor from the Hapsburgs quickly proved to be illusory, for Charles was unwilling and Ferdinand unable to help Hungary.

Charles would not allow the Turkish threat to Hungary and the East to take precedence over his dream for the reestablishment of Christian unity within a new Holy Roman Empire. As Francis I, Henry VIII, and the Papacy opposed Charles' scheme for Hapsburg predominance, it appeared highly improbable in 1521 that his secular aims in the West would be attained in time to assist the beleaguered East.[5]

Charles did nothing to prevent the fall of Belgrade and very little to defend Rhodes. To Adrian's pleas for a two-year truce in the West for the purpose of organizing a crusade against the Turks he answered that he could take no action as long as Francis was undefeated, or until a favorable peace was obtained.[6] Such condi-

---

[3] On the Hungarian situation consult Kupelwieser, *Die Kämpfe Ungarns,* 199 ff.; Merriman, *Suleiman,* 79 ff.; Zarek, *History,* 212 ff.

[4] In 1521 Ferdinand married Anna of Hungary and Louis married Mary of Hapsburg. The marriage contract provided for Ferdinand's succession to the Hungarian throne in the event that Louis had no son. Zarek, *History,* 228–229.

[5] On Charles' aims and foreign policy consult his correspondence with Ferdinand in W. Bauer and R. Lacroix, eds., *Die Korrespondenz Ferdinands I* (Wien, 1912), I, 22 ff., as well as his correspondence with his ambassadors in England and France in W. Bradford, ed., *Correspondence of the Emperor Charles V and his Ambassadors at the Courts of England and France* (London, 1850), 469 ff. The best secondary source is K. Brandi, *The Emperor Charles V* (C. W. Wedgwood, tr., New York, 1939), 13–17, 114 ff. E. Fueter, *Geschichte des Europäischen Staatensystems von 1492–1559* (München, 1919), 250 ff., gives an excellent account of Western reaction to Charles' secular ambitions.

[6] See Charles' correspondence with Adrian in Gachard, *Correspondance,*

tions could not be met; consequently, Adrian's intervention remained futile. Only token help was dispatched by the Emperor after six months of continuous pressure. When Rhodes fell Charles' reaction was one of perfunctory regret. He formally bemoaned the serious loss suffered by Christendom and reiterated his promise eventually to avenge the defeat "para sacrificarla á Dios, si es menester, y por soccorrer y sostener nuestra sancta religion cristiana, como verdadero advogado y protector dessa sancta silla y cabeça temporal de toda la christianidad." [7]

Charles' attitude must have disappointed Louis; indeed, repeated appeals made directly by him or transmitted through Ferdinand were received unfavorably by the Emperor. After 1522 both Louis and Ferdinand sent distress messages to Charles, begging him to conclude an immediate peace in the West and turn eastward to save Hungary from impending disaster, and, in the interim, to send men and money to the hard pressed Hungarians. The Emperor rejected requests for financial aid in view of the large expenditures incurred by him in the West; demands for the conclusion of peace were denied on the pretense that Francis was unwilling to come to terms. Charles was clearly unwilling to alter his own plans for the sake of Hungary; he would, however, promise his assistance once a favorable peace were achieved in Western Europe. [8]

For a short time after the victory of Pavia and the Treaty of Madrid Charles toyed with the idea of helping the Hungarians. [9]

---

52 ff., especially his letter to Adrian of September 7, 1522, *ibid.,* 112–114; also Adrian's letters to Charles beginning with that of September 16, 1522, *ibid.,* 116 ff.

[7] "As a sacrifice to God, if such be needed, and to aid and sustain our holy Christian faith as its true advocate and protector of its holy seat and temporal head of Christendom." Charles to the Duke of Sessa, April 15, 1523, Gachard, *Correspondance,* 178.

[8] In general see Bauer and Lacroix, *Korrespondenz,* I, 17 ff.; K. Lanz, ed., *Correspondenz des Kaisers Karl V* (Leipzig, 1844), I, 66 ff. Louis' and Ferdinand's most eloquent pleas in Bauer and Lacroix, *Korrespondenz,* I, 22 ff. Charles' position is most succinctly stated in his letters to Ferdinand of January 16, 1524 and April 15, 1525, *ibid,* I, 97–98, 105–108.

[9] K. Lanz, *Correspondenz,* I, 66 ff., 168–169.

He wrote the German estates of his desire to fight the Turks. Even the Persian Shah was approached as a possible ally. There were exchanges with Francis on the possibility of a crusade. The peace treaty itself contained a passage expressing determination to battle the Enemy of the Faith. But practical political considerations deterred the Emperor from challenging the Turks at that time. An anti-Turkish war could be hazarded without the cooperation of France and the Papacy; the forming of the League of Cognac was conclusive proof, if such were needed, that no action against the Turks could be taken as long as the Italian question remained unsettled. In 1525 Charles considered Italy more important than Hungary. The Italian wars were resumed and were being fought at the time of the disaster of Mohacs.

Charles' aloofness placed the burden of Hapsburg support for Hungary on Ferdinand, the custodian of his family's interests in Eastern Europe.[10] Unfortunately for Hungary and the Hapsburgs, however, Ferdinand had neither the resources nor the ability to save the kingdom of his brother-in-law.

From as early as 1521 Ferdinand showed grave concern over the Turkish position in Eastern Europe. He realized that the renewed Ottoman aggression, if left unchecked, could bring disaster to Hungary and perhaps even to Germany and the Hapsburgs' Austrian possessions. His frequent letters to Charles, his aunt Margareta, German leaders, and other notables stressed the extreme danger to which Hungary lay exposed, pointing out the precarious position in which the Empire would find itself in the event of Turkish victory in Hungary. Similar arguments were addressed to the German Diets meeting during this period. At least until 1526, Ferdinand believed that Hungary could be saved if aid could be secured; hence, from 1521 until the battle of Mohacs he was a fervent advocate of assistance to Hungary. But where was assistance to be obtained? Not from Charles, for the Emperor was spending

---

[10] Ferdinand's policy is most clearly revealed in his letters and papers contained in Bauer and Lacroix, *Korrespondenz,* vol. I. The most comprehensive, if somewhat antiquated, secondary source is F. B. von Bucholtz, *Geschichte der Regierung Ferdinand des Ersten* (Wien, 1838), I, 135 ff.

his resources in the West. The Hapsburg family possessions were too scanty to contribute effectively to the defense of Hungary. Ferdinand therefore turned to a third source of potential assistance —Germany. This decision, while perhaps ill-timed in view of the German situation in 1521, seemed sound enough as it was based on the tradition established by Maximilian, on the advice of Charles and trusted counselors, and on the exigencies of the Hungarian situation. In light of subsequent developments, its consequences proved far more momentous than the young Staathalter and his advisers could have ever anticipated.

Ferdinand was soon to discover that the German people were unwilling to contribute funds or manpower to preserve Hungary.[11] This was true of the masses, the estates, and even the majority of the intellectuals who only a few years earlier had so enthusiastically supported Maximilian's plans for a crusade. Basically, German coolness to Ferdinand's requests was derived from the almost universal feeling that Germany's problems should have priority over all other issues. However, it also reflected specific attitudes regarding the nature of the Turkish threat and the role that Germany should play in combating it.

In the early twenties, the masses still thought of the Turks as geographically remote, an impression strengthened by their mistrust of imperial motivations. Most Germans believed that appeals for funds against the Turks represented an imperial and papal plot to divert attention from the critical German conditions and enrich the papacy at the expense of the German people. The intellectuals were far more cognizant of the Turkish threat to Hungary as may be seen in the numerous *Flugschriften* published at this time. Yet, despite the dreadful picture of the Turks and their activities limned by the authors of these pamphlets, only a few urged immediate action against the Infidel. The majority stressed the need for settlement of Germany's problems before united and victorious action, under imperial but not papal leadership, should be undertaken by

[11] For general discussions of German reaction toward the Turks see, in addition to the references given in note 13 of Chapter I, R. Ebermann, *Die Türkenfurcht* (Halle a.S., 1904).

all Germans against the Turks. A few adopted an even more conservative attitude, rejecting altogether the idea of an offensive crusade. Their authors, although aware of Hungary's peril, either minimized the danger to the Empire itself, or pointed to the Turks' efficiency as a model for German reform, or accepted the scourge as God's punishment for the sins of Germany and Christianity. To these men fighting the Turks was unjustified except in the event of a direct Ottoman attack on Germany. In this and in some other respects their views were similar to those of Luther, who had repeatedly denounced any offensive against the Infidel, who represented God's punishment for Germany's sinfulness and the wickedness of antichrist, the pope.[12]

Although they differed in content, all *Flugschriften* concurred on the essential point that the Turks constituted no immediate danger to Germany. Even the possibility of Hungarian collapse was not generally envisaged. This appraisal of the situation agreed with that of the *Reichstage* summoned by the Hapsburgs between 1521 and 1526.[13]

In dealing with the German princes and cities, both Charles and Ferdinand, particularly the latter, were confronted with a difficult task. The Diets were unwilling to accede to the Hapsburg requests for assistance to Hungary. Thoroughly suspicious of the Hungarians, they believed that the Hungarian envoys to the German Diets intentionally tried to deceive them; displeased by Charles' indifference to German affairs, they insisted that the Emperor himself make some substantial contribution to any program of aid to Hungary; more interested in the German question than any other, they were not eager to proffer external aid before working out their domestic problems. Moreover, until the disaster of Mohacs the

---

[12] The best general discussion on Luther's views on the Turks is by H. Buchanan, "Luther and the Turks 1519–1529," *Archiv für Reformationsgeschichte*, 47 (1956), 145–160. The specific problem of war against the Infidel is ably treated by G. W. Forell, "Luther and the War Against the Turks," *Church History*, XIV (1945), 256–271.

[13] On the position of the Diets with regard to the Turkish question in the early twenties consult *DRA*, I–IV.

German Diets were not really disturbed over Turkish activities in Eastern Europe.

The princes and cities paid little attention to the demands made by Hungarian emissaries to the Diet which convened at Worms in 1521.[14] Louis' envoys asked for preventive aid in the event of a Turkish attack, stressing the importance of Hungary as a buffer state between Germany and the Ottoman Empire. The estates rejected the Hungarians' plea, questioning the immediacy of a Turkish offensive against Hungary and dismissing altogether the possibility of an attack on Germany. Obviously more concerned with Luther than Louis or Suleiman, the Diet refused to aid Hungary in 1521; it held out, however, the possibility of future assistance should the situation become critical. The Hungarians, without the support of Charles (who seemingly shared the estates' opinion) or Ferdinand (whose position at Worms was inconsequential), had no alternative but to abandon their efforts and again seek aid the following year.

By 1522 the Hungarian situation had worsened, and the Turks had captured Belgrade. The increased danger had been appreciated by Charles as early as August 1521 when he asked the German estates for favorable consideration of Louis' anticipated demands for help. A more urgent message from Ferdinand, requesting the Diet to consider promptly the question of aid to Hungary, followed in the spring of 1522. Influenced by these intercessions, the estates at last recognized the existence of a direct Turkish threat to Hungary, and they listened attentively to the Hungarian delegates whose plans were strongly supported by Austrian and Croatian spokesmen. The clamors for assistance brought no immediate results except for the appointment of a commission to meet in Vienna with representatives of nations threatened by the Turks to determine the extent of the danger and the amount of aid needed. In the interim, the estates made an ineffective attempt to link the Hungarian crisis to the German. The *Reichstag,* anxious to have Charles devote more attention to German affairs, requested the Emperor

[14] The pertinent documents are contained in *DRA,* II, 167 ff.

to conclude a truce in the West and spend more time on the urgent matters of German peace and the Turkish threat to Hungary. The futility of the appeal must have been apparent to the petitioners themselves as they suggested concurrently the alternative solution of their sharing the responsibility for the defense of Hungary with the Emperor. The Diet would send a few thousand men to Hungary provided that Charles would supply whatever additional forces were needed to ensure Hungary's security. In the absence of a satisfactory reply from Charles and because of the suspicions they still entertained regarding the validity of the Hungarian claims, the estates took no decisive action in the spring or summer of 1522. Only after receiving an alarming report from the commission dispatched to Vienna did they agree to send 3,000 men to Hungary. This force was inadequate in terms of Hungarian needs but the Reichstag refused to commit more men.[15]

The position of the German princes and cities on the question of aid had not discernibly changed when the second Diet of Nürnberg met in the fall of 1522.[16] Again the Reichstag refused to grant any substantial assistance in money or men unless Charles would also help or at least consider concluding a truce in the West. The Germans were unwilling to supply an army of 24,000 as requested by the Hungarians, citing adverse conditions in Germany and expressing grave doubts as to the need of so large a force at that time. The maximum contribution they could make would be 4,000 men. Renewed pleas by Hungarian delegates and by a special papal representative only strengthened their inherent distrust of the Hungarians' sincerity. Even a desperate appeal by Ferdinand could not move the estates. Disbelief in the existence of a real Turkish threat coupled with Charles' unwillingness to contribute to the defense of Hungary made them reject Ferdinand's request. Under the circumstances, Ferdinand, who himself had repeatedly failed to persuade his brother to accede to the demands of the German Diets, had no choice but to advise the Hungarians to accept the offer of 4,000 men. He could make no commitment in behalf of the Emperor and had

[15] *DRA*, III, 75 ff.
[16] *DRA*, III, 218–219, 338 ff.

no authority to supply soldiers from the Hapsburg territories. The Hungarians took Ferdinand's advice.

When a new Diet met at Nürnberg in January 1524 the estates were able to detect a slight change in Charles' attitude on the question of assistance to Hungary.[17] This time the Emperor sent one of his ablest emissaries, Joseph Hannart, as his personal envoy to the Diet. Hannart emphasized Charles' predicament in the West and his inability to attend the meeting or send aid at the moment. The Emperor would, however, turn to German affairs and assist Hungary as soon as possible; in the meantime he would have to rely on the Reichstag for the much-needed aid to the threatened kingdom. Ferdinand strongly supported Hannart's appeal, although he would have preferred the conclusion of an immediate truce in the West to free Charles for action in the East. As usual, Hungarian representatives made a dramatic appeal. Their arguments were of a general nature, stressing the standing threat to Hungary, the wickedness of the Turks, and the Mohammedan menace to Christianity; they could not dwell on the imminence of an Ottoman attack since the Turks were then busy harassing the Egyptians. Departing from precedent, the Diet did not challenge the Hungarians' statements, nor did it voice much opposition to the imperial demands. However, the estates reiterated their unwillingness to shoulder the entire burden and their desire for a truce in the West. They even decided to send a delegation to the Emperor to convince him of the necessity of such action. In spite of these token remonstrances, the Diet seemed prepared to consider seriously the aid question.

Charles, supported by Ferdinand, had demanded substantial aid on a continuing basis for the defense of Hungary. The Diet refused to make a long-range commitment but acceded to the imperial demands on a more limited scale. The estates resolved without opposition to grant a rather substantial "emergency aid" amounting to 12,000 foot soldiers and 4,000 infantrymen. Such assistance would continue if the Turkish advance in Eastern Europe jeopardized

[17] *DRA*, IV, 289 ff.

Germany's own security. Moreover, the Diet assured Charles that it would consider the entire question of permanent aid at the next Reichstag which was to meet at Speyer. How can this sudden and surprising shift in attitude be accounted for?

Turkish pressure on Hungary had not increased; the Turks were occupied in Egypt. Moreover, there is no evidence of any changes occurring in the Turkish situation that would have persuaded the estates to alter their earlier stand. Even the towns, traditionally the group most skeptical of need and therefore most ardently opposed to granting assistance, were now in favor of helping the Hungarians. This *volte-face* could hardly have been wrought by the oratory of the Hungarian delegates, whose speeches were comparatively moderate, or by the expectation of endorsement of any plea for aid to Hungary. The most likely explanation is that the Diet was unwilling to refuse Charles.

If the Diet of Nürnberg complied with Charles' request, it was not through fear of imperial sanctions; the Emperor had asked for voluntary contribution which could be freely refused. The cooperativeness of the Diet was based on other considerations. In 1524 Lutheranism, both as a religious and a political movement, was still in its incipient stages. Neither princes nor cities had yet understood the favorable political opportunities created by Luther's teachings. The future leaders of political Protestantism—men like the Elector of Saxony and the Landgrave of Hesse and the free cities of Nürnberg, Ulm, Strassburg, and Augsburg—already showed strong tendencies toward the Lutheran position in religion; none, however, had as yet contemplated political aggrandizement under the aegis of Lutheranism. In fact, in 1524, these early Lutherans were united with the majority of the German Catholics in their desire to bring about a reform in the universal church. Refusing to accept the irreconcilability of Luther's tenets with those of the Catholic Church, blinded by their prejudice against the papacy, most Germans looked upon Luther's activities as representing an impulse toward Church reform. They seemed convinced that a council could achieve this desirable reform, restore the Lutherans to the Catholic fold, and reestablish peace within Germany and Christendom. Peace and religious accord appeared all the more important in 1524 after the Peasant War had undermined the German *Landfriede*. United in aim and supported by Ferdinand, who nurtured the hope that more aid against the Turks could be secured in the event of compliance with the wishes of the Diet, the princes and cities sought the Emperor's consent for their conciliar plan.[18]

It would be difficult to prove that the Diet's complying with Charles' request was due to an expectation that this would induce him to summon a council; in the light of later developments, however, this hypothesis cannot be excluded. Unless it is assumed that the Diet reversed its position from fear of a Turkish invasion of Hungary which might extend as far as a weakened Germany—and the evidence does not justify this theory—there are few other reasons for the estates' approving Charles' request. In fact, upon the Emperor's refusal to summon a council, the Diet reverted to its customary reluctance to follow the imperial lead in matters related to Turkish affairs. In 1524 the expectations of Charles, Ferdinand, and the Hungarians were largely fulfilled; they were to be disappointed, however, at the celebrated first Diet of Speyer which convened in 1526.

On July 15, 1524 Charles rejected the demand for a council, convinced that there was no need to treat with the heretics.[19] In reaching this decision he did not even consider the Hungarian question. It did not occur to Charles that the Diets might force him to alter his stand by refusing to consider requests for assistance against the

---

[18] See Ferdinand's correspondence during this period in Bauer and Lacroix, *Korrespondenz*, I, 84 ff., especially Ferdinand's letters to Charles of June 13, 1524 and October 14, 1524, *ibid.*, I, 177–178, 226; also Charles' letter to Ferdinand of April 15, 1524, *ibid.*, I, 105 ff. In addition, K. Brandi, *Deutsche Geschichte im Zeitalter der Reformation und Gegenreformation* (Leipzig, 1942), 127 ff.; K. Hofmann, *Die Konzilsfrage auf den deutschen Reichstagen von 1521–1524* (Mannheim, 1932), 66 ff.; von Bucholtz, *Geschichte*, II, 37 ff.

[19] On Charles' attitude in 1524 consult Brandi, *Deutsche Geschichte*, 127, 172–173; K. E. Förstemann, *Neues Urkundenbuch zur Geschichte der evangelischen Kirchen-Reformation* (Hamburg, 1842), I, 204 ff.; Hofmann, *Die Konzilsfrage*, 102–104, 111–114; H. Baumgarten, *Karl V und die deutsche Reformation* (Halle, 1889), 5 ff.; Brandi, *Charles V*, 242–243.

Turks before securing concessions on the question of the settlement of religious differences in Germany. Until 1524 the Diets had maintained that conditions within Germany did not warrant a unilateral effort in behalf of the Hungarians, but never totally rejected the imperial requests for aid. Even the towns, the most outspoken critics of Hapsburg policies, never went beyond questioning the proposals for aid submitted to them and reducing specific demands. Luther's followers did not connect the question of aid to Hungary with German religious problems; they offered no objections to the requests of Ferdinand or Charles other than those advanced by the rest of the delegates. In fact, on more than one occasion, the Elector of Saxony urged more aid than that which the Catholic members of the Diet were willing to grant. He supported the imperial policy toward Hungary not as a Lutheran expecting concessions in return but as a German leader convinced of the need to prevent further conquests by the Turks.[20] Before 1524 the religious and the Turkish questions were basically separate issues; however, it was clear to the German Diets that the religious question, though not directly associated with the Turkish one, took precedence over it.

In 1524 a new element was introduced. Both Catholics and Lutherans at the Diet of Nürnberg wished to have the religious question settled by a council but doubted whether the Emperor, who had been insistent on the enforcement of the Edict of Worms, would consent to their request. Therefore, they hoped to secure Charles' approval for their plan by endorsing much of his program for assistance to Hungary. But Charles remained adamant. Convinced of his ability to crush Lutheranism after ending the Italian campaign, the Emperor disregarded the wishes of the Germans and ignored the possible effects of his action on the Hapsburgs' Hungarian projects. The reaction of the estates was unfavorable, as was that of Ferdinand.

In 1524 the Turks did not contemplate an offensive against Hungary; but in 1526, after an indecisive campaign in the Middle East, Suleiman again turned westward. Hungary became the target

[20] *DRA*, III, 242–243; IV, 298–299.

of an intensive attack that started in the summer. Activity along the frontiers alarmed the Hungarians and frightened Ferdinand who in vain appealed to Charles for help. He therefore turned once more to the German estates.

By the summer of 1526 when a new Diet met at Speyer the Hungarian situation had become critical.[21] The Turks were about to launch a decisive campaign against Louis' kingdom, and Ferdinand was gravely concerned. His opening speech to the Diet was an appeal for immediate and substantial aid to Hungary. The Diet, however, was not swayed by his arguments. Angered by Charles' refusal to call a council, the estates declined to consider the question of assistance to Hungary before solving the German religious problem. The Diet appeared determined to solve the religious issues itself, subject to ultimate ratification by a general Christian council to be summoned by the Holy Roman Emperor.

The stand of the estates placed Ferdinand in a difficult position. The Staathalter had instructions from Charles to prevent the settlement of the religious question by a Reichstag, but, at the same time he was dependent upon German aid to save Hungary from conquest. His alternatives were limited: he could either accede to the wishes of the estates or dissolve the Diet. Turkish pressure on Hungary was too great for him to choose the latter alternative; therefore he agreed reluctantly to the former. This was a dangerous concession although Ferdinand was sure that he could keep the negotiations under control. His optimism was based on the belief that, if it became necessary, Charles would agree to a compromise solution of the religious problem in order to clear the way for the granting of aid to Hungary. This appraisal proved essentially correct.

In 1526 Charles himself favored the strict execution of the provisions of the Edict of Worms. He realized, however, that conditions in Germany and Europe precluded the adoption of too intransigent an attitude toward the Lutherans. In Germany, the leaders were united in the desire for the restoration of religious peace by a

[21] W. Friedensburg, *Der Reichstag zu Speier 1526* (Berlin, 1887) is still the only comprehensive treatment of the subject. The documentary section, beginning on page 421, is particularly valuable.

general Christian council. Their wishes could not be entirely ignored at a time when the eastern possessions of the Hapsburgs
were imperiled by an impending Turkish invasion of Hungary and
the Emperor was immobilized in the West by the activities of the
League of Cognac. Under the circumstances, Charles complied with
Ferdinand's suggestion and agreed to the German leaders' demand
for a council. On July 27, 1526 the Emperor authorized Ferdinand
to advise the Diet of his decision to negotiate with Pope Clement
VII with a view to summoning a council.[22]

By the time Charles' instructions reached Ferdinand, the estates
had already received the Staathalter's consent to a discussion of the
German religious question as a preliminary to taking up the Hungarian aid issue. The wisdom of Ferdinand's compromise was
proved by the expeditious manner in which the Diet handled such
matters as questions of dogma, church rites, free preaching of the
gospel, and church organization. Charles' statement was poorly
received by the Diet who considered it too vague; Catholics and
Lutherans alike insisted upon a definite pledge of a council. Ferdinand had no authority to make a more specific commitment on this
matter but because of the gravity of the Hungarian situation he
made a conditional offer to the estates. Faced with the opposition
of the Diet and with the possibility of Hungary's collapsing unless
aid were sent forthwith, the Staathalter promised that a council
would be convened within eighteen months. Moreover, to satisfy
the Lutheran desire for guarantees during this interval, he agreed
to have inserted in the Recess a statement to the effect that "until
the meeting of the council [everyone] would live, act and rule their
subjects in such wise as each one thought right before God and his
Imperial Majesty." [23]

Ferdinand's solution met with the approval of both Catholics
and Lutherans. Thereupon, though doubting the efficacy of assistance at a time when Hungary already lay prostrate, the estates
agreed to send 24,000 men at once to help the Hungarians. This

---

[22] Charles to Ferdinand, July 27, 1526, Bauer and Lacroix, *Korrespondenz,*
I, 408 ff.

[23] Schmauss, *Neue Sammlung,* I², 272 ff.

gesture was of little avail; the Diet adjourned on August 27 and the disaster of Mohacs took place four days later.

Mohacs drastically altered the Hungarian situation. Louis and many of his followers had been killed in battle and Hungary lay open to Turkish conquest. Most of the surviving nobility decided to support Ferdinand's claim to the vacant throne in spite of the Hapsburgs' failure to provide adequate assistance up to the debacle of 1526. They still had enough confidence in his ability to defend Hungary against total Turkish conquest to reject the alternative of supporting John Zápolya, the leader of the anti-Hapsburg faction. As no agreement could be reached between Ferdinand's adherents and those of Zápolya, two rival kings of Hungary were elected. Ferdinand refused to recognize Zápolya who, banking on Turkish support, denied Ferdinand's right to the Hungarian throne. After several months of fruitless negotiations, Ferdinand decided to settle the issue by force.[24]

His determination to become the sole legitimate ruler of Hungary showed a lack of political sagacity, for circumstances were very unfavorable. Neither the Staathalter's Hungarian followers nor the family possessions of the House of Hapsburg could supply the armed force necessary for a strong military offensive against Zápolya plus possible Ottoman supporters. Hence the only course open to Ferdinand was to appeal to Charles and the German Diets for assistance. He sought his brother's aid on the assumption that Charles would appreciate the danger presented by Zápolya and the Turks to the successful implementation of the Treaty of Vienna and the Hapsburg claim in Hungary. He appealed to the Reichstag in the expectation that as Germany's peril was increased by the Turkish victory in Hungary, there would be a corresponding increase in the amount of aid last granted at Speyer. His hopes were to be disappointed.

Repeated appeals to Charles to end the war in the West and come to Ferdinand's rescue were futile. The Emperor refused to abandon

[24] The complexities of the Hungarian situation after Mohacs are carefully worked out in S. Smolka, "Ferdinand des Ersten Bemühungen um die Krone von Ungarn," *Archiv für österreichische Geschichte*, LVII (1879), 1–172.

the war, suggesting instead that Ferdinand reach an understanding with Zápolya until such time as a major Hapsburg offensive could be undertaken against the Turks. He did not share his brother's sense of urgency in 1526 and carefully avoided any action that might precipitate a conflict with the Ottoman Empire.[25]

Ferdinand's appeals to the German estates proved equally ill-timed. In 1526, the imperial administration was forced to make concessions in religious matters because of joint Catholic and Lutheran opposition. Acceptance of the Diet's requests for the convocation of a council paved the way for granting assistance for an apparently lost struggle in Hungary. It is doubtful, however, that the estates made a clear connection between the Turkish threat to Hungary and Ferdinand's interests in that country and the wresting of decisive concessions from the Hapsburgs. To the estates, the securing of an imperial commitment on the summoning of a council was of paramount importance; whether or not a Hapsburg refusal to make concessions would have resulted in outright rejection of Ferdinand's demands for aid against the Turks is open to question. Ferdinand, however, was unwilling to face this possibility at a time of extreme crisis in Hungary; therefore he went beyond the scope of Charles' instructions. On the basis of his action assistance was granted unconditionally by the estates. It is apparent, however, that once concessions were granted and officially recorded in the Recess of Speyer, the estates decided to capitalize on them. The vast majority of the delegates, Catholic and Lutheran, soon sought to secure tangible proof that the Hapsburgs would fulfill their conciliar promises. Dilatory tactics (including activity against the Turks in Hungary) would not be condoned. A similar resolution, differently motivated, was adopted by two Lutheran leaders, the Landgrave of Hesse and the Elector of Saxony.[26] These

---

[25] Ferdinand's correspondence with Charles in Bauer and Lacroix, *Korrespondenz,* I, 450 ff., II, 10 ff.; Charles' replies, *ibid.,* I, 487, II, 62, 109, 120–122.

[26] Among the Lutheran members at the Diet of Speyer only the Landgrave of Hesse and the Elector of Saxony seem to have realized the unlikelihood of final reconciliation between Catholicism and Lutheranism. This belief,

men were the first to realize the implications of the Speyer *Abschied* for the future of Lutheranism. Knowing that a prompt settlement of Germany's religious problems was unlikely, they viewed the moratorium of Speyer as a major gain for their cause, as a basis for expanding the area of religious and political Lutheranism in Germany. One means of safeguarding these gains would be to relate Lutheran interests in Germany to those of the Hapsburgs in Hungary. Ferdinand did not comprehend the effect that the decisions reached at Speyer had in Germany. He anticipated neither the reaction of Hesse and Saxony, nor that of the supporters of the conciliar solution. Optimistically he summoned a meeting of princes at Esslingen, within one month after Mohacs, to consider the Hungarian situation.[27]

At Esslingen the assembled princes acknowledged the seriousness of the Ottoman threat to Hungary but refused to commit themselves on Ferdinand's request to provide generously for the defense of that country against a renewed Turkish attack. Such commitments, they stated, could be made only by the *Ganz Teutsche Nation;*[28] therefore a new Diet would have to be called to act on this matter. Investigations, preliminary to the formal meeting of the Reichstag, were initiated at once.

The attitude of the German leaders at Esslingen and in the months following reflected the changes in German political mentality that had occurred after the Diet of Speyer. No attempt was made to minimize the seriousness of the Hungarian situation. The number of pamphlets devoted to Turkish activities in Eastern Europe had increased considerably since Mohacs. For the most part they painted a dismal picture of atrocities committed in Hungary

---

which they shared at least from 1526, caused them to seek concessions for Lutheranism. On their initiative, the Lutherans obtained the guarantees included in the Recess of Speyer. On these points see Brandi, *Charles V,* 246; Janssen, *History,* V, 287 ff.; L. von Ranke, *Deutsche Geschichte im Zeitalter der Reformation* (München, 1924), II, 312 ff.; T. Brieger, *Der Speierer Reichstag von 1526 und die religiöse Frage der Zeit* (Leipzig, 1909), 68 ff.; Friedensburg, *Der Reichstag,* 410 ff.

[27] *DRA,* VII, 1056–1058; Schmauss, *Neue Sammlung,* I², 281 ff.

[28] Schmauss, *Neue Sammlung,* I², 282.

and the devastation of that Christian kingdom by Infidel armies. They also conveyed vividly the inescapable fact of the Ottomans' proximity to the Empire. Some called for immediate action against the Turks but most expressed the conviction that a united Germany could withstand any attack that might be unleashed against it. The question of Hapsburg succession to the Hungarian throne was ignored by all except the few supporters of Ferdinand who envisioned him as the leader of a German crusade against the Infidel. The general keynote was one of caution: the settlement of Germany's problems was acorded priority over action in behalf of a defeated and divided Hungary.[29]

This prevalent attitude was most concretely expressed by the estates during the discussions preliminary to the Diet of Regensburg.[30] The majority rejected Ferdinand's request for assistance against Zápolya. Most delegates chose to believe the message delivered by Zápolya's envoys to the effect that the Hungarian was a competent Christian ruler, able and willing to defend Hungary against the Turks.[31] Therefore, barring a Turkish offensive directed expressly against Germany, Ferdinand should expect no assistance; instead he should concentrate his efforts on expediting the council promised at Speyer.

A Lutheran minority headed by the Landgrave of Hesse and the Elector of Saxony had more sophisticated reasons for refusing Ferdinand. Eager to preserve the gains achieved at Speyer, they feared to strengthen the Staathalter lest a strong Ferdinand retract the concessions made in 1526. Moreover, they did not wish to support any action that could lead to Zápolya's destruction; Ferdinand's rival might prove useful to the Protestant cause should the Hapsburgs choose to annul the Speyer Recess.[32]

---

[29] The best discussion in Ebermann, *Die Türkenfurcht,* 19 ff.

[30] The pertinent negotiations in *DRA,* VII, 8 ff.

[31] On Zápolya's activities see his letter to Sigismund of Poland, *DRA,* VII, 23; his negotiations with the *Reichstag, DRA,* VII, 26; his instructions to his delegates to the Diet of Regensburg, *DRA,* VII, 976–979.

[32] This attitude seems to have been prevalent among the majority of the six princes and fourteen cities which protested against the Recess of Speyer in 1529. See the letters of Philip of Hesse to Louis of the Palatinate of Feb-

Ferdinand was disappointed in the reaction of the delegates. Realizing that no support could be expected from the estates, he decided, in the spring of 1527, to cope with Hungarian affairs as best he could with whatever forces could be mustered from the Hapsburg family possessions. He could wait no longer; Zápolya had just been formally recognized as King of Hungary by Constantinople. An immediate showdown was essential before he became entrenched in his usurped position. Thus the Staathalter, without support from either Charles or the German estates and despite the probable opposition of the Turks, went to war. Ferdinand's strategy proved effective; Zápolya, unprepared for battle and unable to secure assistance from the Turks in time, was soundly defeated in the fall of 1527. Ferdinand's military victory, however, had to be supplemented by a diplomatic one; securing the sultan's recognition of his claim to the Hungarian throne. He apparently anticipated difficulties as early as the summer of 1527 when he sent his first personal envoy to Constantinople in quest of Ottoman approval. Nevertheless, he hoped that the Turks would recognize the legitimacy of his claim and be favorably impressed by his assurances of peaceful intentions toward the Porte.[33]

Considering the dubious outlook for his mission, Ferdinand decided to capitalize on his victory and consolidate his position in Hungary. This had to be accomplished in the face of a deepening German crisis and Zápolya's renewal of hostilities.

In the summer of 1528 the Diet of Regensburg finally adjourned after formally rejecting Ferdinand's request for assistance in Hungary. Because of the growing strength of Lutheranism since Speyer, the Catholics were now demanding a prompt fulfillment of the

---

ruary 24, 1527 and April 4, 1527, *DRA*, VII, 16–18, 40–41; Philip of Hesse to the Elector of Saxony, February 25, 1527 and April 20, 1527, *DRA*, VII, 22–23, 51–52. On the activities of the Elector of Saxony consult *DRA*, VII, 30 ff.; on the activities and views of the other Lutherans, *DRA*, VII, 2 ff., 937 ff.

[33] A. von Gevay, ed., *Urkunden und Aktenstücke zur Geschichte der Verhältnisse zwischen Oesterreich, Ungern und der Pforte im XVI. und XVII. Jahrhunderts* (Wien, 1838), I², 1 ff.

conciliar promise. Failing this, interim action designed to check the further spread of the heresy was sought from the imperial administration. In any event, Ferdinand could count on no support from the Catholics for the implementation of his policies in Hungary. The Lutherans did not share the Catholic interest in a quick settlement of the religious question; however, they endorsed the decision to withhold assistance to Ferdinand for reasons that were soon to become apparent.

Ferdinand appreciated the response of the Catholics as he himself was increasingly concerned over the progress of Lutheranism in the Empire. He could not, however, abandon the Hungarian campaign until he secured diplomatic recognition from Constantinople. By the fall of 1528 such a possibility appeared remote. The Porte's only reply to Ferdinand's overtures was to give encouragement and military support to Zápolya who began a limited offensive against Ferdinand's forces in Hungary. Zápolya's action augured at best a formal rejection of Ferdinand's plea, perhaps even a major Turkish campaign against the Hapsburgs in Hungary. The likelihood of a showdown with the Turks at a time when the complexity of the German situation was rapidly mounting alarmed Ferdinand greatly. As Staathalter and representative of the Holy Roman Emperor in Germany he had responsibility for German affairs; as heir to Louis' throne he had to protect his interests and succession rights in Hungary. As the success of the latter policy was becoming more and more contingent on his securing assistance from the German estates and as such assistance was in turn contingent on a settlement of the religious question, Ferdinand decided to summon a Diet in November 1528. In view of the precarious German and Hungarian situations, his proclamation stated, the estates were to convene at Speyer on February 2, 1529 to seek a speedy solution for the German religious problem and for the defense of Hungary against anticipated Turkish attack.[34]

While awaiting the opening of the Diet, Ferdinand learned of the Porte's categorical and angry rejection of his plea for recogni-

[34] *DRA*, VII, 1065, 1074–1075.

tion. The Turks (naturally preferring Zápolya to the Hapsburgs) demanded that Ferdinand abandon all succession claims in Hungary and warned him that they would support Zápoyla by military action to prevent further Hapsburg interference in Hungarian affairs. Much of the Staathalter's course of action at Speyer was dictated by the bad tidings which reached him on the eve of the meeting.

When the Diet met Ferdinand urged that substantial assistance be granted for the defense of Hungary until such time as a strong buffer state were established between the Ottoman and Holy Roman empires. At the same time he requested the estates to find a temporary solution to the religious question pending the calling of a council as promised in 1526. These demands were in accord with his immediate interests but not with those of the German estates. The Lutherans, fearing that any settlement of the religious question would limit the scope of the provisions of the generous Speyer Recess, decided to exploit Ferdinand's predicament in Hungary to secure concessions at least as liberal as those granted under similar circumstances in 1526. In reply to Ferdinand's requests they indicated that they would not consider the question of assistance for the defense of Hungary until a satisfactory solution to the religious problem were found.[35] Similar views were expressed by the Catholics, except that the religious settlement they envisaged would restrict rather than liberalize the Speyer provisions.[36]

Because of the irreconcilability of the two positions on the religious question and their determination to make aid against the Turks dependent upon a settlement thereof, Ferdinand tried to separate the issues. The imminence of the Turkish attack on Hungary was cited as the reason for dealing with the question of assistance before seeking even a temporary solution for the thorny religious problem. The Staathalter's urgent request for immediate action could not be ignored by the Diet.

Early in February came increasingly alarming reports of Turkish

[35] *DRA*, VII, 481 ff., 1111. See also J. Kühn, *Die Geschichte des Speyrer Reichstags 1529* (Leipzig, 1929), 42–49, 74 ff.
[36] On the position of the Catholics *DRA*, VII, 414 ff.

movements preliminary to a major offensive. Even the traditional
opponents of German involvement in Hungary agreed that a decisive Ottoman victory there would materially augment the Turkish
threat to Germany. Luther himself reluctantly suggested that fighting the Turks in Hungary could be justified as a defensive measure
and recommended support for Ferdinand's cause.[37] Catholics and
Lutherans alike soon reversed their stands to the extent of granting
16,000 men as temporary assistance to defend Hungary against the
new onslaught. Ferdinand was informed, however, that this concession was dictated entirely by the urgency of the moment, that
no precedent was thereby established, and that under no circumstances would the estates consider his request for long-range assistance until a satisfactory solution had been found for the religious
question. Neither Catholics nor Lutherans wished to separate the
religious and political issues, as both groups realized the tactical
advantages of their linking.

Ferdinand was dissatisfied with the estates' offer, inadequate for
the present and future defense of Hungary, and insisted on reconsideration of his request for *beharrliche Hilfe*. The Catholic
leadership, confident of his support in a showdown with the Lutherans over German affairs, merely restated their earlier position.
The Lutherans, however, seeking to make the Staathalter more
amenable to their wishes for a settlement along the lines of Speyer,
modified their tactics. Their leaders virtually assured Ferdinand
that substantial assistance would be granted as soon as peace was
restored to Germany. Ferdinand would not be tempted by the
Lutherans and agreed to consideration of the religious question
prior to further action by the estates on the defense of Hungary.
Whatever expectations he might have had of agreement between
Lutherans and Catholics were soon dissipated.

The Lutherans were determined to accept no religious settlement
that deviated from the Speyer Recess, and the Catholics were opposed to any solution that would strengthen the position of their
rivals in Germany. The religious problem seemed insoluble. Under

[37] *D. Martin Luthers Werke* (Weimar, 1883–   ), 30^{II}, 86 ff.

the circumstances, Ferdinand adjourned the Diet after approving the Recess which revoked the concessions given the Lutherans in 1526. His demand for long-range subsidies was sacrificed in the process. His action left him in a vulnerable position; the Protestation of Speyer followed.[38]

The Speyer protest, apart from its significance in the German Reformation, carried serious implications for Ferdinand's Hungarian policy. In a last minute attempt to reverse the decisions of the Diet, the "Protestants" refused to abide by their earlier commitment for emergency assistance, claiming that they could not spare any men when their own cause was in danger. They so advised Ferdinand and even Charles, to whom a delegation was sent to seek a repeal of the Recess.

Ferdinand was in a state of consternation. Rumors of the opening of a Turkish offensive had reached Speyer before adjournment; they were confirmed a few days after the Diet had disbanded in May. The aid received at Speyer was deemed insufficient even before the Protestant defection; now it seemed thoroughly inadequate. Moreover, the Staathalter feared a Protestant diversion in Germany while he battled the Turks in Hungary.

Many of his worries proved baseless. The Protestants were not ready to defy the imperial administration in 1529. Charles had sternly told the delegation that decisive imperial action would be taken against the Protestants if they failed to support Ferdinand in his hour of need. The Lutheran leaders were then unprepared to risk such retaliation. Charles was about to conclude the Peace of Cambrai as a prelude to returning to Germany, and the Turks had launched a formidable offensive across the Hungarian plain toward Vienna. Germans, irrespective of religious affiliation, prepared to defend the Empire against the Infidel. All these factors convinced the Protestants that they could not withhold their support, and they participated in the campaign that ended with the Turkish withdrawal from Vienna. Disregarding factional interests,

[38] The division of Germany into two religious camps seemed clear, by 1529, at least to the six princes and fourteen cities which protested at Speyer. *DRA*, VII, 481 ff., 1111 ff.

the Protestants rallied to the defense of the Empire in 1529. But this was the last time that they joined in anti-Turkish hostilities without first securing concessions in religious matters. After the siege of Vienna, Protestantism and the question of assistance against the Turk became more and more closely interrelated.

Before 1529 the leaders of German Lutheranism did not fully take advantage of Ferdinand's need for assistance. Their failure to do so should be ascribed primarily to the fact that the German and Turkish crises concurrently reached a climax only that year. 1529, however, marked the crystallization of tendencies that had first appeared in 1526: a changed Lutheran attitude toward the Turkish threat to Hungary and the exploitation thereof for political purposes.

By 1526 (after the first Diet of Speyer) Philip of Hesse and John Frederick of Saxony had recognized the possibility of utilizing Ferdinand's exigencies to advance the Lutheran cause. But it was only during 1527 and 1528, when the German Catholics and the Staathalter uneasily watched the spread of Lutheranism and sought in vain to arrest it, that Lutheran leaders made a closer connection between the German and Hungarian situations. Hesse and Saxony in particular welcomed Ferdinand's involvement in Hungarian affairs since his absence from Germany facilitated the consolidation and expansion of Lutheranism. They did not, however, wish to assist him lest he feel sufficiently secure to retract the Recess of Speyer. Moreover, Zápolya was regarded as a potentially useful ally if Ferdinand proved refractory.

Their dilemma was solved by Ferdinand himself. His actions in Hungary provoked the Turkish attack of 1529. Faced with mounting German and Ottoman crises, he had summoned the Diet of Speyer. Hesse and Saxony seized their opportunity and they sought reconfirmation of the Speyer *Abschied* of 1526.

The plan of the Lutheran leaders failed not only because the Catholics and Ferdinand opposed concession but also because their policy lacked support among their own followers. As Hesse and Saxony themselves had not yet clearly formulated the principle of "no aid without concessions," they could not convince the majority of the Lutheran delegates—most of whom were ready to help

Ferdinand now that the seriousness of the Turkish threat to Hungary and perhaps even the Empire was undeniable. The "Protestation of Speyer" could not alter the Recess; it was a weak device at a time when the Hapsburgs and the Catholics were firm in their stand against the Protestants and when the majority of the Lutherans were willing to join in the defense of Hungary and the Empire. Only after the policy evolved by the Landgrave and the Elector had been perfected in its details, when it had won extensive Lutheran support, and when the Hapsburg interests in Eastern Europe were in gravest jeopardy could the Protestants obtain concessions by withholding aid against the Turks. This was to be the case in 1532 when the Protestant leaders would achieve their objectives.

Chapter III

The Price of Protestant Aid

The siege of Vienna was not part of a Turkish plan to conquer Germany. It was intended to warn the Hapsburgs that interference in Hungary, the western bastion of the Ottoman Empire, would not pass unchallenged.

Whatever the aims of the Porte, the Ottoman attack of 1529 roused contemporary European leaders to verbal action. Francis I, friendly with Suleiman since 1525, apparently became an ardent advocate of a crusade against his former ally. Charles V promised forceful measures as soon as he had been crowned as Holy Roman Emperor. Even the Pope was to abandon his secular interests in the West long enough to discuss plans for a general crusade with the Emperor during the coronation ceremonies at Bologna. But it was Ferdinand who seemed most concerned over the Turkish advance to Vienna. Discounting the belligerent statements of Charles, Francis, and the Pope as unrealistic in terms of their own objectives in Western Europe, the Staathalter favored peaceful settlement of his differences with the Porte.[1] He hoped that a solution of the Hungarian problem might be reached through negotiation at a time when the Turks had suffered defeat at Vienna and the Western rulers were at least talking about a crusade. A new mission would therefore be sent to Constantinople as soon as feasible to persuade Suleiman to recognize him as King of Hungary. Ferdi-

---

[1] Past, present, and future actions by Ferdinand are indicative of this attitude. A general discussion of Ferdinand's aims and policy in Hungary is contained in von Bucholtz, *Geschichte,* IV, 55 ff. Documents in von Gevay, *Urkunden,* I-III.

nand's ambassadors were to emphasize to the Sultan and the Grand
Vizier Ibrahim Pasha the threat posed to the Ottomans by joint
action of the Christian powers. If such intimidation should prove
ineffectual, the ambassadors were authorized to bribe the Grand
Vizier or to conclude a temporary truce which would give Ferdinand time to strengthen his position with regard to the Turks.[2]

The main reason for the Staathalter's compromising attitude,
apart from his skepticism about the materialization of a crusade,
was the instability of the German situation. Ferdinand knew that
the realization of his ambitions in Hungary depended on German
support, unless the Turks were to yield him recognition either
through negotiation or as a result of a successful military campaign.
But he also knew that after the Turks withdrew from Vienna the
Germans were reluctant to support any further action against them[3]
Although the possibility of eventual resumption of hostilities against
the Empire was not excluded, the Germans did not fear the immediate return of the Turks and were confident of victory in any
engagement with them. The authors of *Flugschriften* and others
who treated the subject of the Infidel agreed that the Empire was
safe from Ottoman conquest, but disagreed as to the wisdom of
supporting Ferdinand's plans for Hungary. Most writers, including
Sebastian Franck, Justus Jonas, and Cochlaeus were still opposed
to supporting any action against the Turks outside the Empire,
deeming the settlement of Germany's problems far more important
than intervention in Hungary.[4] Temporary, perhaps even perma-

[2] Von Gevay, *Urkunden*, I[4], 15 ff., 59 ff.; Ferdinand to Charles, January 28,
1530, Bauer and Lacroix, *Korrespondenz*, II, 580 ff.; von Bucholtz, *Geschichte*,
III, 430 ff., IV, 55 ff.

[3] German opinion may be evaluated through the various *Flugschriften*,
Zeitungen, and songs which appeared during this period. A complete bibliography, with critical comments, may be found in H. Kabdebo, *Bibliographie
zur Geschichte der beiden Türkenbelagerungen Wiens, 1529 und 1683* (Wien,
1876), 1–23.

[4] J. Cochlaeus, *Dialogus de bello contra Turcas* (Leipzig, 1529); *Cronica
abconterfayung und entwerffung der Türckey, von einem Sibenburger in
latein beschriben, durch Sebastian Franck verteüscht* (Nürenberg [?], 1530);
J. Jonas, *Das sibende Capitel Danielis, von des Türcken Gottes lesterung und
schrecklicher mörderey, mit unterricht Justi Jonae* (Wittemberg, 1530).

nent, coexistence was recommended by the most conservative. Few indeed favored taking offensive action at the time. The position of the noninterventionists reflected that of the masses who appeared deaf to appeals from the Pope and others who urged the undertaking of a crusade. Most significantly, however, the German estates seemed confident that the danger to the Empire was over, at least for the nonce.[5] There was general willingness to consider measures for strengthening the Empire's defenses in case of a repetition of 1529, but action would be delayed pending the solution of the religious question. Similar considerations would apply, of course, to the question of giving aid to Ferdinand for Hungary.

The Staathalter himself, aware of the futility of seeking assistance against the Turks prior to attempting settlement of Germany's problems, acceded to the demands of the estates.[6] He was confident that the Porte would be unable to prepare another major offensive for at least a year. During this interval, while Charles was at peace in the West, measures could be taken in Germany, either to enforce the provisions of the Recess of Speyer or, preferably, to seek reconciliation of the conflicting interests by peaceful means. Subsequently, he hoped, assistance against the Turks could be readily secured. Ferdinand had other reasons for according priority to German affairs at this time. Foremost was his dependence on the German electors for approval of his forthcoming nomination by Charles as King of the Romans. Election to that office would notably strengthen his prestige in Germany, Hungary, and even Constantinople. Thus Ferdinand's political future appeared intimately connected in 1530 with prospective negotiations with the German Reichstag and the Ottoman Porte. However, the Staathalter was not a fully independent agent—his policies still required the Emperor's endorsement and support.

[5] In general see Janssen, *History,* V, 241 ff.; G. Mentz, *Johann Friedrich der Grossmütige* (Jena, 1903), I, 69, 74 ff.; J. von Walter, "Der Reichstag zu Augsburg," *Luther Jahrbuch 1930* (München, 1930), 4; H. Virck *et al.,* eds., *Politsche Correspondenz der Stadt Strassburg im Zeitalter der Reformation* (Strassburg, 1882–1928), II¹, 399 ff. (to be subsequently referred to as *P. C.*).

[6] See Ferdinand's correspondence in Bauer and Lacroix, *Korrespondenz,* II, 580 ff.

Charles was in general agreement with Ferdinand's plans.[7] By 1530, having recovered from the initial shock of the Turkish advance to Vienna, he had given up plans for a crusade. Negotiations with the papacy and Francis on this matter proved futile as neither the Pope nor the French monarch would accept Charles' solution of the Italian problems, a prerequisite for joint action against the Turk. Unilateral action was excluded by Charles who still attached greater importance to Italy than Hungary. Nevertheless, the Emperor wanted to help Ferdinand defend his claims to Hungary; he agreed with the Staathalter's insistence that Hungary should not be relinquished to Ottoman domination. Like Ferdinand, Charles now favored a peaceful settlement with Constantinople, provided that Hapsburg interests in Hungary were not sacrificed. He therefore endorsed the aims of the mission that Ferdinand sent to the Porte early in 1530 to negotiate such a settlement.

Charles supported Ferdinand's policy of stressing German affairs for other reasons which differed little from those of his brother. He was anxious to resolve the religious question, preferably through a Reichstag, he wanted long-range support for Ferdinand's Hungarian and Turkish policies, and he was most anxious to have Ferdinand elected King of the Romans.

The choice of a Reichstag as the instrument for restoring peace to Germany instead of a council or military action was dictated by practical considerations. Charles would have preferred a conciliar solution but this was opposed by the Pope and Francis I, who felt it would give too much power to their secular rival by recognizing his claim to imperial supremacy. Agreement might perhaps have been secured through prolonged negotiations but such negotiations would have delayed the settlement of Germany's problems. Speed, moreover, was of the essence as the Emperor feared a renewal of both the Italian wars and Ottoman aggression. Thus, apart from any religious and political considerations related directly to Charles' position as Holy Roman Emperor, a solution in Germany was vital

[7] For Charles' policies after 1529 consult Brandi, *Charles V*, 306 ff.; von Bucholtz, *Geschichte*, III, 430 ff. Charles' correspondence with Ferdinand in Lanz, *Correspondenz*, I, 361 ff.

for the success of his policies in the West and Ferdinand's in the East. Continuing German unrest, leading perhaps to civil war, would certainly be exploited by the foreign enemies of the Hapsburgs and must be avoided.

Charles therefore discarded the conciliar scheme in favor of a Reichstag, particularly as he also entertained the erroneous belief that Protestantism was not solidly entrenched in Germany and that his very appearance at a Diet would so intimidate the Lutherans that they would renounce the "heresy" provided that minor compromises in matters of faith were made. Solution by force was not considered seriously In addition to jeopardizing the successful execution of Hapsburg policies in Europe, it would have hindered the achievement of the third part of Charles' plan: Ferdinand's election as King of the Romans. The Staathalter's election (which would make him actual ruler in Germany and allow Charles to concentrate on Western affairs) depended upon the cooperation of Protestants and Catholics alike. The Emperor wanted his brother elected unanimously to rule over a united Germany which would directly support Ferdinand's policy in the East. For all these reasons the Emperor, acting for himself and his brother, summoned a Diet in the summer of 1530 to "consider the remedies for the said (religious) errors and at the same time provide for and alleviate the evils which were feared on the part of the Turk." [8]

Soon after the opening of the Diet, however, Charles learned that Germany's problems were far too intricate for simple solution.[9] Partly to expedite matters but chiefly to weaken the bargaining

---

[8] Charles V, *The Autobiography of Charles V* (London, 1862), 20.

[9] The imperial policy at the Diet of Augsburg is ably treated by W. E. Mayer, "Forschungen zur Politik Karls V während des Augsburger Reichstages von 1530," *Archiv für Reformationsgeschichte,* 13 (1916), 124 ff. The pertinent documents for the *Reichstag* in general will be found in K. E. Förstemann, *Urkundenbuch zu der Geschichte des Reichstages zu Augsburg im Jahre 1530* (Halle, 1833–1835), I, 201 ff., II, 1 ff. See also "Die Depeschen des Venezianischen Gesandten Nicolo Tiepolo über die Religionsfrage auf dem Augsburger Reichstage 1530," J. von Walter, ed., *Abhandlungen der Gesellschaft der Wissenschaften zu Göttingen* (Philologisch-historische Klasse), Neue Folge, XXIII (1928), 1 ff., for an astute contemporary appraisal.

position of the Protestants, the Emperor requested in his opening address that the less complex questions of assistance for the defense of Hungary and the Empire and the election of Ferdinand as King of the Romans precede consideration of the religious question itself. The estates, unwilling to place all the trumps in Hapsburg hands, immediately rejected this. Neither Catholic nor Protestant was deceived by Charles' transparent stratagem. Both sides attached supreme importance to prompt consideration of German issues and their negotiating tactics, particularly those of the Protestant leaders, were to be linked closely if necessary to the matters that Charles wanted summarily settled. Defeated in his original tactical mancuver, the Emperor agreed to immediate consideration of the outstanding religious problems.

Once more Charles was disappointed. Within a short time it became apparent that his sanguine expectations of settling the religious differences at a Reichstag would not be realized. The Protestants were uncompromising in their theological tenets as embodied in the Augsburg Confession, and the Catholics refused to make concessions on fundamentals. With discussions reaching a stalemate, the Emperor reconsidered his original plan. Two choices were open: to seek solution of the religious problems at a general Christian council or to secure the assistance of the Catholics for a war against the Protestants. The former alternative had the support of Ferdinand and the German estates, the latter of the papacy. The Emperor himself vacillated. While leaning toward a conciliar solution, he had grave doubts that any council would be able to reconcile the conflicting positions. As he also questioned the likelihood of any council assembling in the near future, he began to toy with the idea of using force to bring the Lutherans to heel. The papal envoys to the Diet had consistently advocated such a step, urging that the moment was propitious for decisive action. They assured Charles of papal cooperation and tried to assuage his fears of the Turks or French exploiting an armed clash in Germany by emphasizing their unpreparedness.

Charles was tempted, but he was unable to secure the cooperation of the Catholic estates. The German Catholics mistrusted the papacy and would consider military action only as a last resort. A council alone could bring about the much needed reform of the Roman Church, they stated; once this were achieved the Lutherans would rejoin it voluntarily. The Emperor could not ignore the wishes of the Catholics as he needed their support both in his struggle with the Lutherans and for the fulfilment of his hopes for anti-Turkish appropriations, as well as for the election of Ferdinand as King of the Romans. He therefore reconfirmed the conciliar solution.[10]

Charles' willingness to attempt settlement of the German religious problem by means of a council did not imply a retreat from the fundamental position expressed in the Recess of Speyer of 1529. The Emperor would submit only theological problems to the council and allow no innovation in matter of faith until the council met. In the interim he expected the Lutherans to rejoin the Catholic Church and thereby stabilize the German situation.

This unrealistic scheme for the temporary solution of Germany's problems was submitted to the Diet for discussion just as negotiations on the questions of assistance against the Turks and Ferdinand's election were getting underway. The Emperor, counting on Catholic support, was prepared to force the issue despite certain Protestant opposition to his conciliar plan and other demands. In this he was momentarily successful. The initial imperial request called for substantial assistance, on a permanent basis, for the protection of Hungary and Germany against the Turks.[11] This demand was given tentative consideration during the late stages of the religious debates but was formally rejected after brief deliberation. Neither Catholics nor Lutherans were willing to give up their traditional opposition to long-term commitments until the German question was settled. When the Emperor's formula for treating the religious problem became known, the Catholics pressed for

---

[10] His letter, summarizing his position, to García de Loaysa, October 20, 1530 in Mayer, *Forschungen,* 71–72.

[11] For negotiations on and other matters related to the question of assistance against the Turks consult Förstemann, *Urkundenbuch,* II, 109; von Walter, *Depeschen,* 66 ff., 82 ff.; *P. C.,* II¹, 462 ff.; Schmauss, *Neue Sammlung,* I², 322 ff.

consideration of the alternate imperial request for emergency assistance. Gratified by Charles' proposals in matters of religion, the Catholic estates declared their readiness to offer aid for the defense of the Empire. Most Lutheran delegates adopted a similar course in the hope that their cooperation might soften the Emperor's insistence on their reentering the Catholic fold. Only the Protestant leaders did not share the optimism of their coreligionaries. Instead of banking on Charles' goodwill they were thinking in terms of assurances. Believing that the Emperor, supported by the Catholics, could secure Reichstag approval for his religious pacification plan, they wanted guarantees of immunity from retaliatory action in the event of continued Lutheran nonconformity. They advised Charles that whatever aid they might grant against the Turk would be contingent upon their receiving such assurances. Charles' answer was sufficiently equivocal to satisfy the majority of the Lutheran estates who joined the Catholics in granting 40,000 infantry and 8,000 cavalry for the specific purpose of defending the Empire should it be threatened by Turkish attack. The Protestant leadership, though more skeptical of Charles' intentions than the body of the Lutherans, yielded to the decision of the majority. Obviously no advantage could be gained by withholding aid under the circumstances.

Having secured what the Hapsburgs felt was adequate emergency aid, Charles concentrated on the last aspect of his program: Ferdinand's election. He soon received promises from all electors except the Protestant John Frederick of Saxony that they would cast their votes for the Staathalter.[12] The Emperor now declared himself satisfied with his achievements at Augsburg. Perhaps overconfident about what seemed to be a major political success, Charles chose to disregard the Saxon Elector's threats to vote against Ferdinand and those of the Protestant leaders to withhold delivery of the granted aid against the Turks until definite guarantees of nonaggression were given them by the imperial administration. Rely-

[12] On this point see particularly Mayer, *Forschungen,* 124 ff., with the pertinent documents beginning on page 133, bearing on Charles' plan to secure a non-protested election for Ferdinand.

ing on Catholic support for its enforcement, Charles approved the drastic Recess of the Diet of Augsburg.[13] The Augsburg Confession was rejected and April 15, 1531 was set as the date by which the Lutherans were to rejoin the Catholic Church pending final settlement of matters of faith by a council. The highest court of the Empire, the *Kammergericht* (Imperial Chamber), was granted extraordinary powers to enforce the provisions of the Recess and particularly to prevent further territorial expansion of Lutheranism in Germany. These powers, though judicial in character, could be implemented by Catholic military action.

Stringent as these terms were, the decisions reached at Augsburg did not constitute a victory for Charles. Within a few weeks after adjournment it became evident that the Augsburg decisions could not be enforced. The Lutherans had been unable to prevent the proclamation of the Recess of Augsburg because of the close cooperation between the Emperor and Catholics in a period of relaxation of international pressures on the Hapsburgs, but they now sought to recoup their losses by exploiting the needs and weaknesses of their opponents. Protestant strategy became manifest shortly after the Diet ended and Charles left Germany.[14] In December the Elector of Saxony voted against Ferdinand; in February 1531 the League of Schmalkalden was formed; in April the Protestant leaders refused to supply the aid granted for the defense of the Empire against the Turks unless Charles officially guaranteed them immunity from Kammergericht action until the calling of a council. The Protestants were striking back at the Recess of Augsburg; they were developing a technique for insuring the continued existence, even expansion, of Lutheranism in Germany.

Saxony's refusal to recognize Ferdinand as King of the Romans, a device later utilized by the Schmalkaldians, was designed to prevent such centralization of authority as might facilitate the enforcement of the Recess of Augsburg. It also served as a lever to

---

[13] Schmauss, *Neue Sammlung*, I², 322 ff.

[14] The best, if somewhat dated, discussion of Lutheran reaction to the Recess of Augsburg is by O. Winckelmann, *Der Schmalkaldische Bund 1530–1532 und der Nürnberger Religionsfriede* (Strassburg, 1892), 60 ff.

secure concessions from the Hapsburgs. The League of Schmalkalden, ostensibly formed for defensive purposes, constituted in effect the nucleus of Lutheran forces determined to prevent destruction of their creed. Lastly, the Protestants' refusal to pay the aid granted at Augsburg represented a clear formulation of the doctrine of "no aid without concessions." The Protestant course was based on a well-calculated risk in view of rapidly changing German and European conditions.

Charles left Germany apparently determined to enforce the decisions of Augsburg.[15] He would make no concessions to the Protestants but would seek papal agreement for the summoning of a council with all possible dispatch. He also requested his brother to expedite his Turkish negotiations, for agreement with the Porte would strengthen Ferdinand's hand in dealing with the Protestants. Charles' illusions were soon dispelled and the necessity of compromise with the German Protestants became a harsh reality in the late spring of 1531.

The Emperor was unable to win over the Pope, influenced by Francis, to a conciliar solution of Germany's religious problem. Ferdinand's envoys in Constantinople had been unsuccessful. In May they secured a tenuous truce on the basis of the *status quo,* but Ferdinand's claims to Hungary had been indignantly rejected. The news from Germany was disturbing. As expected, the Protestants tried to sabotage the Recess of Augsburg, but worse, defections from the Catholic camp were reported. The Bavarian Dukes, William and Louis, traditional opponents of Hapsburg aggrandizement in Germany and Eastern Europe, had joined the Schmalkaldians in refusing to recognize Ferdinand as King of the Romans. Ferdinand was desperately pressing for a compromise with the Protestants; indeed he had repeatedly advocated a modification of the Augsburg Recess.[16] He seemed particularly concerned over the Protestants' defaulting on their grant of aid against

[15] Brandi, *Charles V,* 317 ff. Winckelmann, *Schmalkaldische Bund,* 90 ff.

[16] Ferdinand's position is most clearly expressed in his correspondence with the Emperor: Lanz, *Correspondenz,* I, 442 ff.; von Gevay, *Urkunden,* I⁴, 97 ff., I⁵, 3 ff.

the Turks and the unholy alliance formed between Bavarians and Schmalkaldians, whom he feared might seek the help of Francis and Zápolya to deprive him of his throne.[17] His fragile truce with the Porte might be dissolved at any time. He needed peace in Germany to secure his position as King of the Romans and strengthen himself against a possible renewal of hostilities in Hungary. All these factors, intensified by a gradual weakening of the precarious peace in the West, made a reevaluation of the Augsburg stipulations advisable.

Nevertheless, Charles hesitated.[18] His own inclinations were to adhere to the provisions of the Recess. The international and German situations were not sufficiently critical, he thought, to warrant entering into immediate negotiations with the Protestants without first making further efforts to win Clement VII's assent to the conciliar plan. He was also encouraged by the attitude of the majority of the German Catholics who opposed concessions to the Lutherans. He could not ignore, however, the existence of a moderate Catholic group, headed by the electors of Mainz and Pfalz, who favored temporary suspension of the integration provisions pending final resolution of the problems at a council.

Finally the Emperor yielded to the pressure of the forces favoring compromise and agreed to undertake negotiations with the Lutherans for the purpose of altering the Recess of Augsburg.[19] On June 8 he convoked a Reichstag for September 14 at Speyer to work out a religious truce in Germany until a council could meet.

---

[17] Ferdinand's fears were unfounded as his opponents did not contemplate an alliance with Zápolya or Francis I in 1531. On these points consult Winckelmann, *Schmalkaldische Bund*, 82 ff.; M. Doeberl, *Entwickelungsgeschichte Bayerns* (München, 1908), I, 410 ff. See also Ferdinand's correspondence in von Gevay, *Urkunden*, I⁴, 103 ff., and Lanz, *Correspondenz*, I, 426 ff.

[18] For Charles' attitude consult Brandi, *Charles V*, 320 ff.; also his correspondence in Lanz, *Correspondenz*, I, 424 ff. A good general discussion of the situation in Germany after Augsburg may be found in A. Westermann, *Die Türkenhilfe und die politisch-kirchlichen Parteien auf dem Reichstag zu Regensburg 1532* (Heidelberg, 1910), 4 ff.

[19] The most lucid explanation for his decision is found in Charles' letter to his wife of July 13, 1531, Brandi, *Charles V*, 325–326.

The imperial terms were rigid. Charles would recognize the existing territorial limits of Lutheranism but would retain the provisions of Augsburg prohibiting further expansion. He would, however, allow suspension of measures designed to reintegrate the two faiths until the meeting of the council. In return for the concessions he was prepared to make, he would expect the Protestants to fulfill their Augsburg commitment for aid against the Turks and to provide such assistance as might be required in the future, to recognize Ferdinand as King of the Romans, and to live in active allegiance to himself and his brother. These conditions were conveyed to the Schmalkaldians in July by the Emperor's personal emissaries, the Counts of Nassau and Niewenar, sent to pave the way for the impending discussions.[20]

The Schmalkaldians found the terms unacceptable.[21] In their reply they demanded cessation of all Kammergericht action against the Lutherans. Charles in turn rejected this proposition which he and the majority of the Catholics felt was extreme. Supported by the Catholics and encouraged by the fact that the international situation had at least not deteriorated since July, Charles was emboldened to discontinue his preliminary negotiations with the Protestant leadership. He decided in order to strengthen his bargaining position to initiate intensive negotiations with the Catholics to form a common front against the Lutherans and with the Turks to consolidate their recent truce with Ferdinand. If these goals could be achieved, he hoped then to force the Lutherans to adopt his program. The Emperor postponed the meeting of the Diet to gain time for the realization of these schemes. The Reichstag was now to meet on January 6, 1532 at Regensburg. But Charles was not successful in his preliminary maneuvers. When the assembly opened in January the advantage was clearly on the side of the Lutherans. The shift was due to the renewal of Turkish hostilities against the Hapsburgs.

[20] Charles' instructions to his envoys to Germany, the counts of Nassau and Niewenaar, July 1531, Lanz, *Correspondenz*, I, 512–516.

[21] Details on the preliminary negotiations may be found in the documentary section of Westermann, *Die Türkenhilfe*, 175 ff.

This new international crisis was provoked by Ferdinand.[22] Instead of pursuing a cautious policy toward the Turks at a time when Charles was engaged in delicate negotiations in Germany and a mission had been sent to the Porte in accordance with Charles' wishes, the elected King of the Romans sought to gain further strategic advantages against the Schmalkaldians, the Bavarian Dukes, and especially Zápolya. Acting on the erroneous assumption that the Turks would not risk a major war with the Hapsburgs over a localized struggle between himself and Zápolya, Ferdinand attempted to seize the stronghold of Ofen in the fall of 1531. Its capture, he thought, would strengthen his position in both Hungary and Germany. Victory over Zápolya would give him control of a key strategic area; it would also discredit the Hungarian usurper as a potential ally of the Schmalkaldians and the Bavarian Dukes, and perhaps even frighten his German opponents into recognizing him as King of the Romans.

His foolhardy plan proved disastrous. The attack on Ofen was a fiasco and resulted in the abrupt termination of Hapsburg-Ottoman negotiations by the Porte, who also promised immediate military retaliation for such a breach of the truce of May 1531. This left Charles little choice but to seek resumption of discussions with the Protestants. On January 10, 1532 he advised the Schmalkaldians of his decision to renew the negotiations interrupted the previous summer.[23] On February 7 he stated his revised terms to the Protestant leaders. In return for Lutheran observance of the *Landfriede,* contribution of aid against the Turks, abstention from further religious proselytizing among the Germans, and recognition of Ferdinand as King of the Romans, Charles was prepared to accept the Confession of Augsburg as valid until the meeting of a council and to recognize the existing territorial limits of Lutheranism until that time. The door was left open for compromise when the Emperor

---

[22] For Ferdinand's policies in Hungary and his relations with the Porte consult von Gevay, *Urkunden,* I[5], 68 ff. Von Hammer, *Histoire,* V, 154 ff., is the best source on Ottoman policy.

[23] Charles' instructions to Pfaltz and Mainz, von Bucholtz, *Geschichte,* IX, 28 ff.

indicated his willingness to discuss the entire question of German peace with the Protestant leaders either at the Diet of Regensburg or some other place in the vicinity of that city, preferably Nürnberg.

The Schmalkaldians, though not satisfied, agreed to accept Charles' plan as a basis for further discussion.[24] A counterproposition was presented to the Emperor by the Protestant leadership which had met at Schweinfurt at the end of March 1532 to formulate the Lutheran terms. Seeking to exploit Charles' predicament with a major Turkish offensive imminent, the Schmalkaldians demanded repeal of the Augsburg Recess, abolition of the Kammergericht and other secular and religious concessions that were tantamount to recognition of Protestantism in Germany. Accession to the Emperor's demands (including, of course, assistance against the Turks) would be contingent upon his accepting their conditions. Charles found the Protestant price exorbitant but agreed to continue the negotiations. Indeed, he could not break them off because of the inescapable fact that an adequate defense of the Empire would be impossible without Lutheran cooperation.

However, on the basis of his conferences with the Catholics, he expected their delegates at Regensburg to endorse his terms vigorously. He also hoped that they would grant enough assistance against the Turks to minimize his reliance on Lutheran support. Such actions, combined with intimidation or persuasion of the Lutheran rank and file at the Diet, should force the Schmalkaldians to revise their extravagant demands. This apparently well-conceived strategy failed.

The Diet which opened at Regensburg on April 17, 1532 proved less cooperative than the Emperor had expected.[25] The delegates

[24] Detailed chronological accounts of the negotiations of 1532 may be found in A. Engelhardt, "Der Nürnberger Religionsfriede von 1532," *Mitteilungen des Vereins für Geschichte der Stadt Nürnberg*, XXXI (1933), 17 ff., 28 ff.; Westermann, *Die Türkenhilfe*, 59 ff.; Winckelmann, *Schmalkaldische Bund*, 195 ff. Documentary material is contained in Westermann, *ibid.*, 172 ff.; *P. C.*, II², 120 ff.; J. Ficker, ed., "Aktenstücke zu den Religionsverhandlungen des Reichstages zu Regensburg 1532," *Zeitschrift für Kirchengeschichte*, XII (1890–91), 583 ff.

[25] Documents in Westermann, *Die Türkenhilfe*, 172 ff.

could not be budged from the position taken by their leaders at
Schweinfurt. The Catholics, regardless of differences among themselves or with the Hapsburgs, opposed even a discussion of the
Schmalkaldian terms, generally insisting on the enforcement of the
Augsburg Recess. However, they refused Charles' request for substantial assistance against the Turks which, if granted, would have
greatly enhanced the Emperor's bargaining position with the Protestants. The conservative majority justified the Catholic attitude by
pointing at Ferdinand's unwarranted attack on Ofen, at the Hapsburgs' excessive reliance on German assistance (best exemplified by
Charles' apparent unwillingness to assign his own forces to the defense of Hungary and the Empire) and by questioning the imminence or seriousness of a Turkish attack on Germany. The Catholics,
therefore, declined to raise the appropriation made at Augsburg
two years earlier; moreover, their offer was made conditional on
Charles' matching it. Of course, the Emperor got no comfort from
the Lutherans who refused to give *any* assistance until the Augsburg Recess was revised.

The Diet of Regensburg's attitude toward the Turkish question
forced Charles to act. On May 6, with rumors rife that vast Ottoman
forces had left Constantinople, he made a counteroffer to the
Schmalkaldian demands for *de facto* recognition: to license limited
preaching of Lutheran doctrine outside present Protestant areas and
to rescind the corresponding powers of the Kammergericht. A few
days later the Schmalkaldians rejected the Emperor's proposition,
reiterating their earlier demands. Thereupon, Charles requested
that direct negotiations be suspended until June 3 to permit further
consideration of the Protestant demands. They were resumed at
Nürnberg under circumstances favorable to the Emperor.

In view of the intransigence of the Schmalkaldians, Charles decided late in May to renew his attempts to secure adequate assistance
against the Turks from the Diet of Regensburg. He pointed out to
the estates that Turkish forces had actually left Constantinople on
April 25, reportedly headed toward Hungary. Stressing the inevitability of an attack on the Empire itself, he promised to subsidize a considerable military force from his own personal funds.

He pleaded with Catholics and Lutherans to contribute liberally, and was rewarded by unexpected cooperation from the Lutherans.

As soon as a major Ottoman offensive against the Empire appeared probable, the uncompromising attitude of the Lutheran estates at Regensburg began to change. Gradually delegates indicated willingness to grant aid for the defense of Germany without relation to the modification of the Augsburg Recess. This apparent schism in the Lutheran ranks encouraged Charles to restate on June 8 his offer of May 6 to the Schmalkaldians at Nürnberg. The Protestant leaders, conscious of their weakened bargaining position but still aware that Charles would have to compromise with a Turkish attack impending, again rejected the Emperor's terms. However, as they were under pressure to share in the imperial defense, they agreed to revise their demands.[26] The Schmalkaldians' counteroffer made allegiance to the Hapsburgs, recognition of Ferdinand and, above all, assistance against the Turks contingent upon Charles' recognizing the territorial *status quo* in Germany and suspending all Kammergericht action until the meeting of a council. The Emperor considered the Schmalkaldian proposal worthy of further discussion. He was anxious to stabilize the situation in Germany before the Turk struck. The Protestant demand would have to be modified, however, in view of his own unwillingness to invalidate the secular provisions of the Augsburg Recess and inevitable Catholic opposition to a compromise along the lines desired by the Schmalkaldians. He therefore decided to prepare his reply in consultation with the Catholic estates at Regensburg.

The Emperor found the majority of Catholic delegates firmly opposed to any compromise with the Protestants. Convinced that

[26] Engelhardt, *Der Nürnberger*, 93 ff.; Westermann, *Die Türkenhilfe*, 88 ff., 142 ff.; Winckelmann, *Schmalkaldische Bund*, 237 ff. German fear of a major Turkish offensive against the Empire is also revealed in various *Flugschriften, Zeitungen,* and songs. See, for instance, *Kriegsruestuge unnd Heerzuegt des wüterichen Türckischen Keysers* (n.p., 1532); *Copey unnd lautter Abschrifft ains warhafftigen Sendtbrieffs wie der Türkisch Kayser Solyman disen sein yetz gegenwürtigen Anzug wider die Christenheit geordnet von Constantinopel aussgezogen* (n.p., 1532); *Ein Sermon vo dem Turckenzug* (n.p., 1532). Also consult von Liliencron, *Die historischen,* IV, 50–57.

the Lutherans at Regensburg as well as the Schmalkaldians at
Nürnberg would soon grant unconditional aid against the Ottomans, they urged abandonment of all negotiations with the Protestant leaders and a reconfirmation of the Recess of Augsburg.
Thereupon, fearing that in time Charles might be swayed by the
Catholic arguments and that the Lutheran delegates would indeed
grant aid unconditionally with the Turkish threat mounting, the
Schmalkaldians took the initiative by gratuitously promising assistance for the defense of the Empire.[27] This partial capitulation
was made on the assumption that Charles was still anxious to
achieve his goals in Germany and would not risk a Protestant
defection.

The Schmalkaldian strategy succeeded. Indeed, the Emperor was
too concerned over the Turkish threat and too doubtful of the
realism of the Catholic viewpoint to dare to abandon negotiations
with the Protestant leaders.[28] Despite Catholic opposition, he repeated his offer of June 8 on July 7. The Schmalkaldians accepted
it in principle and after tense discussions on the proper formulation
of the final terms, a formal agreement, the Religious Peace of
Nürnberg, was reached on July 23. According to this agreement,
the Emperor acknowledged the territorial *status quo* until the calling of a council and agreed to cessation of Kammergericht action
in spiritual but not secular matters until that time. In return the
Lutherans agreed to observe the *Landfriede* and give their whole-
hearted allegiance to Charles, as Holy Roman Emperor, and Ferdinand, as King of the Romans.[29] The German Catholics refused to
acknowledge officially the terms of the agreement or to include them
in the Recess of Regensburg of July 27.[30] They chose to regard the
Religious Peace of Nürnberg as a personal arrangement between
the Emperor and the Protestants, as a *fait accompli* which they

---

[27] Westermann, *Die Türkenhilfe,* 223 ff., 231–232; *P. C., II²,* 153.
[28] As late as June 25, 1532 Charles was convinced that the Protestants would
not cooperate unless they would first secure a satisfactory religious peace.
Ficker, *Aktenstücke,* 594.
[29] Engelhardt, *Der Nürnberger,* 109 ff.
[30] Schmauss, *Neue Sammlung, I²,* 353 ff.

could not reject when the Empire was in danger of invasion but which they could later challenge.

Ultimately, the forebodings over the anticipated Ottoman offensive proved groundless. While it is true that within two weeks of the adjournment of the Diet of Regensburg, in early August, the Turks were reported within eleven leagues of Vienna and a siege of that city seemed inevitable, the same Turks were stopped at Güns by a garrison commanded by one Nicholas Juricic.[31] On August 28, with autumn approaching, Suleiman ordered his forces to return to Constantinople. After raiding Styria the Turkish armies turned homeward by mid-September. All these developments, however, could not have been known before August 1532 and by then the Lutherans had obtained concessions that proved of profound significance in the future. In fact, the terms of Nürnberg formed the rallying point of Protestant demands for almost ten years and were of primary importance for the survival, expansion, and consolidation of Lutheranism in Germany.

The events and decisions of the period dating from the withdrawal of the Turks from Vienna in 1529 to their return in 1532 were highly significant for German Protestantism. They were conditioned, to a considerable extent, by the conflict between Hapsburgs and Turks in Hungary and by fear of Ottoman action against the Empire itself.

In 1530 the subsiding of the Turkish threat to the Empire and the possibility of temporary reconciliation of the conflicting Hapsburg and Ottoman interests in Hungary facilitated the adoption of the severe Recess of Augsburg. However, the proximity of the Turks to the imperial boundaries and their declared hostility to long-range Hapsburg interests in Hungary acted as a deterrent to any military clash between Charles and the Lutherans. These factors also affected enforcement of the Recess of Augsburg. If the instability of political conditions in Western Europe, papal opposition to a conciliar solution of Germany's religious problems and dissension among German Catholics were considerations behind

[31] Charles to Maria of Hungary, August 13, 1532, reporting that the Turks were within eleven miles from Vienna. Lanz, *Correspondenz*, II, 3.

Charles' decision to reach a peaceful understanding with the Protestants in 1531, so was Ferdinand's insistence on the compromises necessary to achieve German unity, and the Emperor's sharing of his brother's apprehensiveness toward the unyielding and ever-menacing Porte. But, regardless of which factors weighed most heavily in 1531, those connected with the Turkish threat were decisive during the final stages of the negotiations between Emperor and Protestants in 1532. Indeed, Charles' concern over the prospect of a divided Germany facing what purported to be an overwhelming Turkish offensive compelled him to conclude the Religious Peace of Nürnberg. Its terms embodied concessions that the Protestants had wrested from the Emperor by exploiting the Hapsburgs' need of assistance in defending their interests in Hungary and within the Empire itself.

The gains of the Protestants at Nürnberg were considerable. Charles had recognized Lutheranism as an established religious and political movement with well-defined territorial limits. He had also agreed to the teaching of the Lutheran dogma outside these limits. But the Protestant leadership still was not content. The Religious Peace of Nürnberg was a temporary agreement in effect only until a council met. It still retained the *Kammergericht* as an instrument for preventing the territorial expansion of Lutheranism. Most significantly, it was not officially recognized by the Catholics. These were serious disadvantages which the aggressive Protestant leaders intended to lessen or eliminate as soon as possible.

The decade following the second Turkish attack against the Empire would bring continuous Protestant attempts to broaden the provisions of the Nürnberg agreement by removing all restrictions on the expansion and consolidation of Lutheranism in Germany. Exploitation of an expanding conflict between Hapsburg and Turk continued to be the instrument of that policy.

Chapter IV

Hapsburg Policy between Turk and Protestants

The failure of the second Turkish attack on the Empire and the inevitability of conflict with the bellicose Shah Thamasp of Persia made it advisable for Suleiman to renew his 1531 armistice with Ferdinand. In the spring of 1533 the Sultan advised the King of the Romans of his willingness to conclude a treaty of "perpetual peace" on the basis of the *status quo* in Hungary. As an inducement Suleiman would permit direct negotiations between Ferdinand and Zápolya on the question of succession. Should the King of the Romans persuade the King of the Hungarians to abdicate in his favor, the Sultan would consent.[1] Ferdinand resented this subterfuge, knowing that the Hungarian would never voluntarily renounce his throne;[2] nevertheless, he did not reject the Ottoman peace offer and his counterproposal demanded outright recognition as King of Hungary. But the familiar arguments presented by special envoys (Hieronimus of Zara and Cornelius Scepperus) failed to move the Porte; therefore the original Turkish terms

---

[1] Von Gevay, *Urkunden*, II¹, 3 ff.; von Hammer, *Histoire*, V, 179 ff.; Zinkeisen, *Geschichte des Osmanischen Reiches*, II, 738 ff.

[2] For Ferdinand's policies toward the Porte and Zápolya in 1533 and 1534 consult von Gevay, *Urkunden*, II¹, 30, 84 ff., 138–139, 149 ff.; W. Friedensburg *et al.*, eds., *Nuntiaturberichte aus Deutschland 1533–1559* (Gotha, 1892–1912), I, 81, 99, 101, 166, 169, 240, 270, 279 ff. (to be subsequently referred to as *N. B.*). H. Kretschmayr, "Ludovico Gritti," *Archiv für österreichische Geschichte*, LXXXIII (1896), 55 ff., is an excellent account of the complexities of Eastern diplomacy in this period.

formed the core of the "perpetual peace" treaty concluded at Constantinople in June 1533.

Ferdinand welcomed the news of the agreement and also the approaching Turkish involvement with the Shah. He hoped to take advantage of quiescent conditions in Germany to prevail upon Zápolya to give up his crown. With Suleiman's consent he opened direct negotiations with him in the fall of 1533. Zápolya, however, supported by the Sultan's representative, Ludovico Gritti, refused all concessions and the negotiations dragged on.

While Ferdinand bided his time until the Turkish offensive began in the Middle East, Philip of Hesse, with the tacit approval of the Schmalkaldian League, was plotting an anti-Hapsburg coup in Würtemberg.[3] This would be a flagrant violation of the Religious Peace of Nürnberg, but the Landgrave was prepared to accept the risk. Würtemberg belonged to Ferdinand, and Ferdinand, he thought, would be willing to give it up in exchange for the consolidation of his authority in Germany and support for his Hungarian plans. Hesse, with Schmalkaldian consent, would offer the King of the Romans terms that should be irresistible. The Protestant leaders would recognize the validity of his claims to Hungary and support his policies to the extent of granting subsidies for strengthening Hungary's defenses against the Turks. They would also formally recognize Ferdinand as King of the Romans in accordance with the yet unexecuted stipulations of the treaty of Nürnberg. These provisions should allay Ferdinand's fears of a possible alliance between the Schmalkaldians and Zápolya and also assure the Protestants of immunity from the Kammergericht proceedings sure to follow the seizure of Würtemberg. As King of the Romans, Ferdinand could halt any punitive action initiated by the Catholic-controlled Imperial Chamber.

Hesse's scheme proved successful. In the summer of 1534 he took Würtemberg and restored the Lutheran Duke Ulrich to power. The Schmalkaldian terms, presented simultaneously to Ferdinand, were indeed irresistible. Despite Catholic protests and threats of unilateral

---

[3] The best general accounts of Hesse's activities and German affairs in this period are still Janssen, *History*, V, 397 ff.; von Ranke, *Deutsche Geschichte*, IV, 52 ff.

retaliatory action, Ferdinand and the Schmalkaldians quickly concluded the Compact of Cadan.

The magnitude of the Protestant victory was limited only by Catholic refusal to recognize the Cadan agreement. Repeating the tactics of 1532, they regarded the Compact as a personal treaty between Ferdinand and the Schmalkaldians. Kammergericht proceedings would be initiated, not against Philip of Hesse or Ulrich of Würtemberg (since Ferdinand had ratified their action), but against the Lutherans in Würtemberg who were not protected by the Religious Peace of Nürnberg. The Catholics would follow procedures used since 1532; they would try to halt the spread of Lutheranism through judicial action against all new converts outside the territorial limits recognized by Charles at Nürnberg.

The Catholic interpretation of Cadan and enforcement of the Nürnberg provisions, although objectionable in their long-range implications, did not cause immediate concern to the Protestant leadership in 1534. The Catholic estates that could have enforced the decisions of the Imperial Chamber by military force were loath to do so. Their hesitancy reflected both continuing confidence in a successful conciliar solution of Germany's problems and fear of precipitating a showdown with the Protestants without Hapsburg support. The Schmalkaldians knew that neither council nor support would be forthcoming very soon. They had tied Ferdinand's hands at Cadan while Charles was immobilized by the maneuvers of the Turks, the French, and the papacy.

In 1534 the Emperor was faced with new problems created by the activities of the Ottoman fleet in the western Mediterranean. Incursions into Spanish territorial waters, begun in the late twenties, increased in frequency and intensity. In 1529 the corsair Khaireddin Barbarossa raided Algiers. This action marked the beginning of regular naval warfare between the Spanish and Ottoman fleets. The element disturbing to Charles was not the strength of the Turkish squadrons, whose activities were successfully countered by the Spanish under Andrea Doria's command, but the realization that the Ottomans were receiving cooperation from Francis I.[4] Indeed, a

---

[4] Documents pertinent to Franco-Turkish relations in this period may be found in Charrière, *Négociations*, I, 247 ff. See also Ursu, *La Politique*, 56 ff.

Franco-Turkish *rapprochement* had taken place shortly after the waning of Francis' crusading zeal in 1530 and would have led to a formal anti-Hapsburg alliance had it not been for the second Turkish campaign against the Empire which forced the Most Christian King to temporize again. Secular interests, however, proved stronger than spiritual considerations and in 1533 Francis renewed his friendship with the Sultan. The French action coincided with Charles' attempt to end the Mediterranean warfare by peaceful means.[5] The Emperor had asked Suleiman to broaden the "perpetual peace" with Ferdinand by including all areas of conflict between Hapsburg and Turk in the treaty. But the Sultan, encouraged by the French monarch, refused. He could not forgive Spain's humiliation of the Moors and would not free Charles to support a possible coup in Hungary or to war against his friend Francis during his own absence in Persia. Rather would he intensify the war in the Mediterranean.

In March 1534 Suleiman appointed Barbarossa *Kapudan Pasha* (admiral) of the Ottoman fleet and ordered the seizure of Tunis. After ravaging the coasts of Sicily and southern Italy, Barbarossa complied with the command in the fall of that year. Thus alerted, Charles began to prepare himself for a full-scale combat in the western Mediterranean.[6] The Turkish action coincided with renewed French intrigues in Italy and Francis' overtures to the Bavarian Dukes and German Protestant leaders in search of alliance against the Hapsburgs. Charles followed the course anticipated by Hesse and his associates. In the spring of 1535, on the eve of a campaign that would result in the reconquest of Tunis and the destruction of much of Barbarossa's fleet, the Emperor sent Adrian of Croy to Germany to reassure the Protestants of his peaceful intentions.[7] Charles' envoy advised the Protestants that the Emperor

[5] In 1533 and 1534 Charles had sent ambassadors to the Porte to seek a truce. Von Gevay, *Urkunden,* II¹, 46, II², 3 ff.

[6] Documents pertinent to relations between Charles and the Porte in von Gevay, *Urkunden,* II², 3 ff. and Charrière, *Négociations,* I, 247 ff. See also Brandi, *Charles V,* 348 ff.

[7] Charles' instructions to Adrian of Croy in C. Weiss, ed., *Papiers d'Etat du Cardinal de Granvelle* (Paris, 1841–1852), II, 337 ff.

had agreed to confirm the Compact of Cadan and reconfirm the Nürnberg agreement, assuming continued Protestant loyalty to the Hapsburgs. He emphasized, however, the temporary nature of these concessions, reminding them of Charles' determination to persist in his conciliar efforts. While acknowledging the futility of such attempts during the pontificate of Clement VII, he expressed the hope that the new pope, Paul III, might be persuaded to summon a general Christian council in the near future.

Heartened by the turn of events, the Schmalkaldians sought to extend their gains the following year when conditions seemed particularly propitious.

The year 1536 recorded major setbacks for Hapsburg policies in Europe. In the spring, Francis and Sulciman finally concluded a formal alliance against the Hapsburgs.[8] The Sultan, returning to Constantinople after an inconclusive campaign in the Middle East, was easily convinced of the advisability of united action against the common enemy. Ottoman prestige, Francis argued, had been damaged by Thamasp's successful stand against the Turkish armies, by Charles' reconquest of Tunis and victory over Barbarossa, and by Ferdinand's maneuvers to replace the Sultan's protégé, Zápolya, in Hungary. The new allies soon took the offensive in the West by intensifying Francis' and Barbarossa's hostile activities, in the East by *de facto* repudiation of the treaty of "perpetual peace" between Ferdinand and the Porte.

Francis' provocative actions stemming from his desire to possess Milan and his unwillingness to evacuate Piedmont and Savoy clashed with Charles' determination not to allow changes in the Italian clauses of the Peace of Cambrai. A new Italian war between the two broke out in the summer of 1536 and was accompanied by new western Mediterranean raids by the rebuilt Turkish fleet. Ferdinand was also under pressure from the Turks. Suleiman, impelled

---

[8] On the significance of the alliance and its impact on Hapsburg policies see Fueter, *Europäischen Staatensystems,* 300 ff.; Brandi, *Charles V,* 347 ff.; Kretschmayr, "Gritti," 81 ff.; Zinkeisen, *Geschichte des Osmanischen Reiches,* II, 817 ff. Valuable documentary material in Charrière, *Négociations,* I, 255–263, 283–294.

by his own interests as well as by his alliance with Francis, reasserted his authority in Hungary. He had little to fear from Ferdinand as long as Zápolya kept faith with him. But in the fall of 1534 the Turkish representative Ludovico Gritti was mysteriously assassinated and suspicion grew that the act was connected with an anti-Turkish conspiracy involving the Hapsburg and the Hungarian. To discourage a compromise between the Christian rivals and to support the aims of his alliance with Francis, Suleiman ordered a renewal of hostilities against the King of the Romans. They assumed the form of minor incursions into Slovenia and Croatia beginning in the summer of 1536. More serious action could be anticipated after the Ottomans had fully recovered from the effects of the Persian campaign.

It was at this point that the Protestants made their move. Emboldened by the Hapsburg predicament, the Schmalkaldians dispatched a mission to Charles at Nice to request revision of the Religious Peace of Nürnberg.[9] They asked that the powers of the Imperial Chamber be curtailed and the privileges granted the Lutherans in 1532 be extended retroactively to all new converts. Because of the international situation, the Emperor could not summarily dismiss the Protestant appeal. He was opposed, however, to liberalizing the terms of the Nürnberg agreement, rightly fearing that further concessions would invalidate its original purpose. But he was equally anxious to avoid an outright rejection of the Schmalkaldian demands at a time when the maintenance of harmony in Germany was mandatory.

The imperial strategy was formulated accordingly.[10] Confronted with this new Protestant request, Charles accelerated negotiations already in progress with Pope Paul III on the convening of a council. The Pope, requiring Charles' support for the realization of his secular ambitions in Italy, was ready to accede to the Emperor's urgings on a *quid pro quo* basis. He could afford such a concession, knowing that a council, even if summoned, would not sit immedi-

---

[9] The most comprehensive survey of Schmalkaldian policies in this period is by Janssen, *History,* V, 440 ff.

[10] Charles' policies are admirably set forth in Brandi, *Charles V,* 371 ff., 400 ff.

ately. The Italian war and Francis' opposition alone precluded this. Therefore Paul III ordered a general Christian council to assemble at Mantua in May 1537.

Charles welcomed the papal gesture although he himself doubted its sincerity. But the possibility of a council could be held like the sword of Damocles over the heads of the German Protestants. The Emperor advised the Schmalkaldians that he would send his chancellor, Mathias Held, to Germany to investigate conditions and seek an equitable solution to the problems there. In December 1536 Held arrived in Germany, carrying flexible instructions from his master.[11]

The chancellor's objectives were to insure the maintenance of the *status quo* in Germany and to secure assistance from the estates for the defense of Hungary and for Charles' war against the Infidel in the West. He was to urge the Lutherans to attend the Council of Mantua but should reemphasize Charles' determination to abide by the Nürnberg agreement until May 1537 or, in the event of postponement, until the council actually did meet. These assurances were to be given even if the Protestants refused to attend the council. Finally, Held was empowered to take any *ad hoc* measures that would facilitate the achievement of these basic imperial aims.

The choice of Mathias Held was unfortunate, for the chancellor was too loyal a Catholic and too inflexible a diplomat to maintain the precarious *status quo* and secure Protestant support for the secular policies of the Hapsburgs. In fact, instead of stressing the conciliatory aspects of Charles' instructions, his actions increased the instability of the German situation and prevented the granting of assistance against the Turks.

Upon arriving in Germany, Held avoided direct communication

---

[11] Charles' instructions to Held in Lanz, *Correspondenz*, II, 268–270. On the Held mission consult G. Heide, "Nürnberg und die Mission des Vizekanzlers Held," *Mitteilungen des Vereins für Geschichte der Stadt Nürnberg*, VIII (1889), 161 ff., and, by the same author, "Die Verhandlungen des kaiserlichen Vizekanzlers Held mit den deutschen Ständen (1537–1538)," *Historisch-politische Blätter für das katolische Deutschland*, CII (1888), 713 ff. A good general discussion of Charles' relations with the Protestants from 1537 to 1539 may be found in W. Rosenberg, *Der Kaiser und die Protestanten in den Jahren 1537–1539* (Halle a.S., 1903), 1 ff.

with the Protestant leaders. Instead he conveyed Charles' wishes individually to the more conservative Lutheran cities in an attempt to weaken the collective negotiating power of the Schmalkaldian League. Held was able to ascertain in this way that the Protestant cities would not attend the Council of Mantua, which they considered "unfree" but would send representatives to a free council and consider the Emperor's request for assistance. Interpreting this answer as an indication of Protestant weakness, the chancellor requested the Schmalkaldians in February 1537 to attend the council and to grant substantial subsidies against the Turks. He bluntly added that no changes in the Religious Peace of Nürnberg would be made in view of the impending meeting at Mantua.[12]

The Protestant leaders rejected Held's demands.[13] They reiterated the arguments of the cities in refusing to attend the council and refused Charles' requests for aid, emphasizing their traditional opposition to supporting offensive action outside Germany. However, they agreed to reconsider the question of assistance if the Emperor would reconsider his stand on their demands of 1536. Held would not accept these conditions and the negotiations were broken off. The chancellor did not try to make use of the loophole in the Protestant rejection of his original request by mentioning Charles' decision to abide by the provisions of Nürnberg under all circumstances. His attitude was based on a growing conviction, derived from his discussions with the Lutheran cities and the Catholics, that nothing could be gained by appeasing the Protestants. Doubting that any Protestant aid would be worth the price demanded, he withheld the conciliatory reassurances of the Emperor. Believing that the Protestants were vulnerable, giving an appearance of strength merely because the Catholics were weak and the Hapsburgs indecisive, Held thought the situation called for a forceful policy. Only through an uncompromising approach to negotiation

---

[12] Heide, *Nürnberg und die Mission des Vizekanzlers Held,* 170 ff., 185 ff.; K. Lanz, ed., *Staatspapiere zur Geschichte des Kaisers Karl V* (Stuttgart, 1845), 248.
[13] The Protestant position in *N. B.,* II, 128 ff.; *P. C.,* II², 429 ff. See also G. Mentz, *Johann Friedrich der Grossmütige* (Jena, 1903–1908), III, 357 ff.

and show of military strength could the progress of Lutheranism be arrested. Held not only broke off negotiations with the Schmalkaldians but also laid the foundations for a Catholic league, similar to that of Schmalkalden, designed to defend Catholic interests against Protestant aggression. His actions, while eminently justified from a Catholic standpoint, deepened the German crisis and, paradoxically, strengthened the Protestant cause.

The basic aim of Protestant policy since 1532 had been to retain and expand the provisions of the Religious Peace of Nürnberg. This treaty, despite its unilateral and revokable character, offered basic guarantees sufficient to ensure the continuing existence of Protestantism. But the document had never been officially recognized by the Catholics and did not provide for changes in the *status quo.* It offered no sanctions against violation of its provisions by the Catholics, did not legalize Lutheran expansion in Germany, nor did its protection extend to new converts. During the four years that had elapsed since the conclusion of the agreement, the Protestants had tried to have these deficiencies corrected, but with no sense of urgency until the arrival of the Held mission.

The Schmalkaldians were satisfied with a policy of unilateral toleration as long as their interests were not threatened by revocation of the document or flagrant violation of its terms. As long as Charles abided by its provisions, as long as a council (which would automatically terminate it) did not meet, and as long as the Catholics were too weak to interfere seriously with their policy of expansion, the Protestant leaders did not press the issues of official recognition or extension of the provisions of the Religious Peace of Nürnberg. However, with the prospect of an imminent council meeting and a Catholic military organization which would strengthen the authority and enforcement powers of the Catholic-controlled Kammergericht, the Protestants decided to intensify their efforts to gain legal recognition in Germany.[14] They began by seeking concessions and guarantees from the Hapsburgs that

[14] On Protestant reaction to Held consult Lanz, *Staatspapiere,* 255 ff.; Mentz, *Johann Friedrich,* 357–358; *P. C.,* II², 429, 441, 445–446 note 3, 473, 485, 490, 498–499, 508.

would force Catholic recognition of a substantially broadened Nürnberg agreement.

Similar plans had been tentatively considered by several members of the Schmalkaldian League before 1537. Its general acceptance and implementation of the policy, however, became possible only after Held had revealed to the Schmalkaldians the insecurity of their position. Legal recognition was in fact not achieved until twenty years later, although the struggle began in earnest in 1538. Ferdinand's need for aid against the Turks gave the Protestant leaders their opportunity to extract the important concessions they had planned.

In the fall of 1537 Ferdinand, encouraged by the lack of organized Turkish activity in southeastern Europe but disturbed by the continuous raids of the Pasha of Bosnia into southern Hungary, ordered General Katzianer to undertake a punitive expedition against the Bosnian. Katzianer's forces were easily defeated but the aggressive action provoked the Porte, who accelerated his preparations for war against Peter Rareş, the ruler of Moldavia, who was regarded as a potential ally of the Poles and Hapsburgs. War seemed imminent in the spring of 1538.

The prospect of an organized Turkish offensive in the late spring or summer alarmed Ferdinand who suspected that the move might be directed against Hungary as well as Moldavia. His anxiety was shared by Zápolya. The Hungarian knew that the assassination of Gritti had undermined the Sultan's confidence in him to such an extent that Suleiman might well contemplate his replacement now. Zápolya therefore decided to negotiate an agreement with Ferdinand at a time when both feared Turkish reprisals. In February 1538 Zápolya and Ferdinand signed the Treaty of Grosswardein. In return for Hapsburg protection against Turkish attack, the Hungarian agreed to recognize Ferdinand as his successor. This agreement precipitated a major Turkish attack on Moldavia which started in the late spring.

The likelihood of the war's expanding into Hungary caused Ferdinand to seek immediate assistance against the Turks from the German estates.[15] He could not meet his obligations toward Zápolya in any other manner as his own resources were insufficient and Charles was heavily committed in the West. But his urgent pleas were of no avail. The Catholics, encouraged by Held, refused to grant aid unless German conditions were stabilized to their satisfaction; the Protestants flatly refused their support unless definite guarantees were given them at a Reichstag. Ferdinand believed that a compromise might be reached in time to overcome the joint opposition to his request for aid against the Turks. Assuming that the Catholics would refuse to settle their differences with the Lutherans by direct negotiation but wouldn't oppose an agreement similar to the Religious Peace of Nürnberg, Ferdinand decided next to ascertain the extent of the Protestant demands. Negotiations were begun in the early summer with Joachim of Brandenburg serving as mediator between the King of the Romans and the Schmalkaldians.[16]

The Protestant demands were framed along the lines of their appeal to Charles of 1536. The Lutheran leaders requested extension of the peace of Nürnberg to all who had joined their faith since 1532, abolition of Kammergericht action against these new converts, and official recognition of these terms by a Reichstag. In return, they would immediately grant substantial emergency aid against the Turks. They would also consider the question of permanent subsidies for Hungary at the same Diet that ratified the concessions they now demanded. Should these terms be acceptable to Ferdinand, they requested that he and the Emperor send plenipotentiaries to a meeting between the Schmalkaldians and the Hapsburgs in order that a preliminary understanding might be reached as soon as possible.

Ferdinand did not reject the Protestant demands. While unacceptable as formulated, he thought that they might be amended

---

[15] For Ferdinand's policies and the attitude of the German estates consult *N. B.*, II, 110 ff.; *P. C.*, II², 473 ff. Good secondary accounts in von Bucholtz, *Geschichte*, IV, 141 ff.; P. Fuchtel, "Der Frankfurter Anstand vom Jahre 1539," *Archiv für Reformationsgeschichte*, 111–112 (1931), 145 ff.

[16] *N. B.*, IV, 468–469.

sufficiently to form the basis of an agreement. He therefore referred them to Charles, whose consent was needed for any change in the Religious Peace of Nürnberg. Underlining the new Turkish threat, he urged sympathetic consideration of the Protestant offer.[17]

However, Charles was not inclined to compromise in the summer of 1538.[18] He had just concluded with Francis the Truce of Nice and would soon meet the French king at Aigues Mortes. He envisaged lasting peace in the West and an opportunity to resolve both his conflict with the Turks and the German question. Then he would concentrate his forces on expelling the Turkish fleet from the Mediterranean and assembling a *bona fide* council in lieu of the impromptu and indefinitely adjourned meeting of Mantua. Therefore, he would not conclude any new agreement with the Protestants. At most he would reconfirm the provisions of the Nürnberg agreement until a council was assembled—and this only because of the Turkish situation. Charles appreciated Ferdinand's need for assistance in Hungary which he himself could not provide because of his commitments to Venice and the papacy (which had joined him in the Holy League) to destroy Barbarossa's fleet. He also entertained the idea of a joint Hapsburg offensive, by land and sea, against the Porte; this could not be undertaken without German support. For these reasons alone Charles consented to send a plenipotentiary as requested by the Schmalkaldians and desired by Ferdinand. In November 1538 he appointed the Archbishop of Lund in that capacity and armed him with instructions that would disappoint both Ferdinand and the Protestants.[19]

While awaiting Lund's arrival, Ferdinand, unaware of Charles' terms, continued his negotiations with the Protestant leaders through his intermediary Joachim of Brandenburg.[20] The King of

---

[17] Ferdinand to Charles, August 1, 1538, *N. B.,* IV, 450; Ferdinand to Joachim of Brandenburg, November 21, 1538, *N. B.,* IV, 487–488.

[18] For Charles' policies consult Brandi, *Charles V,* 416 ff.; also Lanz, *Staatspapiere,* 263 ff.; *N. B.,* IV, 454 ff.

[19] Charles' instructions to Lund, *Correspondenz,* 277–281.

[20] Ferdinand to Joachim of Brandenburg, November 2, 1538 and January 18, 1539, *N. B.,* IV, 487–488, 504–505.

the Romans appeared willing to consider the demand for extension
of the Religious Peace of Nürnberg to new converts and to reach
an understanding on Kammergericht action. He would remove the
most objectionable members of that body and seek clearer distinc-
tions between spiritual and temporal cases. The Schmalkaldians
were encouraged by Ferdinand's conciliatory offer which they
realized was engendered by his fear of the Turks. They therefore
agreed to continue negotiations along these lines at the meeting of
plenipotentiaries which was to assemble at Frankfurt in February
1539.

When the Protestants met with Lund and Ferdinand's plenipotentiaries at Frankfurt they presented demands that far exceeded
their original terms, requesting the conclusion of an agreement that
would officially and permanently recognize Lutheranism as an
organized religion in Germany.[21] They expected all rights and
privileges pertaining to an officially recognized religion, including
free propagation of its beliefs and the right of every German to
change religious affiliation without fear of reprisal. Naturally, all
activities of the Kammergericht in matters of faith had to end and
Lutherans, now with legal status in Germany, should be appointed
as well as Catholics to a reformed Imperial Chamber. Lund immediately rejected the Protestant terms. Revealing his instructions,
he asserted that the Emperor would not conclude any new long-
term agreement. Such action would be superfluous in view of
Charles' decision to seek a definitive solution to the religious con-
troversy as soon as feasible. He would, however, reconfirm the terms
of the Religious Peace of Nürnberg in the interim and embody these
guarantees in a formal document. In return for these concessions,
the Emperor would expect the Protestants to grant aid against the
Turks as requested by Ferdinand and to send representatives to a
meeting of Catholic and Lutheran theologians which Charles would
convene within the next few months to attempt the reconciliation

---

[21] On the Frankfurt negotiations consult *N. B.*, III, 500 ff., IV, 507 ff.
Fuchtel, *Der Frankfurter*, 167 ff., provides an intelligent interpretation of the
discussions at Frankfurt.

of differences in dogma. This meeting would be preliminary to the holding of a council.

The Protestant leaders at once rejected Lund's proposition, but presented a counteroffer of their own. They would settle for temporary instead of permanent recognition for a period of three to five years provided that all other demands were met. Only under these circumstances would they grant aid against the Turks. Lund refused to consider the Protestant terms, reiterating his previous proposal. After stormy negotiations the Schmalkaldians agreed to moderate their demands. In return for extension of the Nürnberg peace to those who had joined the Lutheran ranks since 1532, suspension of Kammergericht action in matters of faith for not less than eighteen months, and the issuance of formal guarantees that the Catholics would respect these provisions, they would give favorable consideration to the request for subsidies against the Turks. Under pressure from Ferdinand who thought that the Protestant demands were sufficiently reasonable, Lund agreed reluctantly to consider them as the basis of a formal agreement. On April 19, 1539 such an agreement was actually concluded, subject to Charles' approval.[22] The provisions of the Religious Peace of Nürnberg would be extended to all who turned Lutheran between 1532 and 1539 until the meeting of a council, general or national, and Kammergericht action would also be suspended until that time. The Hapsburgs would protect the Lutherans against violation of these terms by the Catholics for a period of not more than fifteen months and not less than six. In return, the Protestants agreed to obey the *Landfriede,* to send theologians to Nürnberg by August 1 to seek preliminary reconciliation of doctrinal differences with the Catholics, and to attend a general *Türkentag* at Worms on May 18 to grant subsidies against the Turks.

Protestant retrenchment from the extravagant demands of February 15 to the moderate terms of April 19 was an inevitable consequence of a shift in bargaining positions that occurred during this period. When the Schmalkaldians formulated their demands

---

[22] J. J. I. von Döllinger, ed., *Beiträge zur Politischen, Kirchlichen und Cultur-Geschichte der sechsletzten Jahrhunderte* (Regensburg, 1862), I, 16–22.

during the winter 1538–1539, the Turks were still threatening
Hungary, and Charles and his allies were engaged in battle with
the Turkish fleet in the Mediterranean. Naturally these circumstances affected the extent of the Schmalkaldian demands. But
counterforces were already at work when the Protestant leaders
met with Lund and Ferdinand's envoys at Frankfurt. The strin-
gency of Charles' terms awakened doubt in the Schmalkaldian
camp as to the Emperor's intentions. Might he not support the
Catholics if the Protestants insisted on their terms? This possibility
seemed a remote one at the time because of Charles' involvement
with the Turks, but it could materialize once that conflict were
over. The bargaining position of the Schmalkaldians was further
weakened by dissension among Lutherans over the granting of aid
to Ferdinand. Should the Turks indeed undertake a major offensive
against Hungary (which might again lead to an invasion of the
Empire), no doubt the Lutheran estates would respond as they
had under similar circumstances in 1529 and 1532.[28] But another
alternative also occurred to the Protestant leaders: the distinct possibility that the Turkish armies, partly disbanded after driving Rareş
from Moldavia the previous summer, might not be ready for a new
offensive in 1539. In either case concessions would have to be made.
It was for these reasons that the Schmalkaldians agreed to modify
their intentionally inflated demands in February. As time progressed
the Schmalkaldian position became increasingly untenable. Like
Held, Lund soon became aware of the relative weakness of the
Protestants. He understood the Schmalkaldian dilemma regarding
Charles and the Turks. He also learned from discussion with the
Catholics that they would oppose any compromise with the Lutherans. Denouncing Charles' and Ferdinand's conciliatory attitude
toward the Protestants, the Catholics insisted that a general council
be assembled as soon as possible; otherwise a Reichstag, acting as
a national council, would have to settle Germany's problems. The
spread of Lutheranism must be stopped. The Catholic attitude

---

[28] Several Lutheran estates had expressed readiness to support Ferdinand as
early as the summer of 1538 should the Turkish threat assume serious proportions. *P. C.*, II², 508, 510–511, 567.

strengthened Lund's determination not to deviate from Charles' instructions despite Ferdinand's more generous terms of 1538. It did not, however, affect the tactics of the Schmalkaldians who could disregard Catholic opposition as long as the Hapsburgs were inclined to compromise. What ultimately caused the Protestants to moderate their demands was a change in Ferdinand's attitude resulting from the waning of the Turkish threat to Hungary and the hardening of Catholic demands for final settlement of the German question. This change occurred in March when news reached Germany that no spring campaign was contemplated by the Porte.

The removal of the immediate Ottoman threat to Hungary strengthened Catholic opposition to Hapsburg policies. The Catholic League threatened defiance of any agreement that might be reached between Hapsburgs and Protestants at Frankfurt and reemphasized, in the name of the Catholic estates, the need for settling Germany's problems as soon as possible. Lund agreed with the Catholics, reassuring them of Charles' intentions. But the Catholics sought similar assurances from Ferdinand. The King of the Romans immediately thought of a compromise satisfactory to all. He would limit concessions to the Schmalkaldians to his offer of 1538, persuade Lund to accept them as the basis of a temporary agreement and appease the Catholics by acceding to their demands for speedy action on the settlement of the German issues. Ferdinand was willing to take all these measures for the sake of German peace and subsidies against the Turks. The relaxation of Turkish pressure on Hungary was at best temporary, he believed, and it should be exploited to consolidate the Peace of Grosswardein and strengthen Hungary's defenses.

Through adroit maneuvering Ferdinand achieved most of his aims.[24] Although the Schmalkaldians at first refused to reduce their demands to the level desired by the King of the Romans, they ultimately agreed to make the necessary concessions when they realized that Ferdinand could not be swayed from his limited com-

---

[24] Ferdinand's tactics are trenchantly analyzed by the papal nuncio Aleandro in *N. B.*, IV, 521 ff. See also Ferdinand's letter to Lund of March 27, 1539, *N. B.*, III, 513–515.

promise offer. As Catholic pressure against any agreement mounted and Lund's stand on keeping all concessions within Charles' original offer remained unshaken, Ferdinand issued an ultimatum to the Schmalkaldians. Thereupon, the Schmalkaldians presented their drastically revised demands. While these still exceeded the limits of his proposal of 1538, the King of the Romans was too much tempted by the prospect of assistance against the Turks to reject them. Instead he was able to amend them sufficiently to secure Lund's conditional acceptance and persuaded the Schmalkaldians that his changes, including the stipulations regarding the settlement of Germany's religious problems, were essential to prevent outright rejection of a final agreement by Charles and the Catholics.

The Schmalkaldians accepted the revised terms and their incorporation into the Frankfurt *Anstand,* but with serious misgivings.[25] Their dissatisfaction stemmed less from the extent of the concessions wrung from Ferdinand than from the tenuous nature of the agreement itself. Extension of the provisions of the Religious Peace of Nürnberg and suspension of Kammergericht action would indeed have constituted major gains in the Protestant struggle for recognition had they not been so severely limited in time and subject to imperial ratification. Favorable action by Charles was necessary to validate the concessions included in the agreement and ensure their observance by the Catholics. The Schmalkaldians seemed confident that a formal acceptance of the Frankfurt Anstand by the Emperor would prevent the Catholics from defying its terms and thus permit the Protestants to formulate and implement policies that would consolidate and further the gains realized in 1539. But grave doubts were voiced in the Schmalkaldian camp as to whether Charles would approve the agreement. The concessions ultimately recorded departed completely from the Emperor's instructions and Catholic opposition to them had been more violent than anticipated by Ferdinand. Would Charles side with Ferdinand or with the Catholics, whose first reaction was to denounce the agreement and in-

[25] The Schmalkaldian attitude after Frankfurt can be evaluated best from the documents contained in *P. C.,* II², 602 ff., and *N. B.,* IV, 520 ff. See also Fuchtel, *Der Frankfurter,* 192 ff.

tensify Kammergericht proceedings against the Lutherans? The only barrier to the latter alternative was Charles' war against Barbarossa, and that conflict did not seem sufficiently important to force the Emperor to consent to Ferdinand's terms.

In accordance with this reasoning, the Schmalkaldians drew up a course of action designed to secure *de facto* if not *de jure* approval of the concessions won at Frankfurt. Essentially, it entailed increasing Ferdinand's dependence on Protestant assistance, appeasement of the Catholics and direct appeals to the Emperor.

On May 18 at Worms the Protestants retracted their promise to grant subsidies against the Turks. They advised Ferdinand that Charles' failure to ratify the Frankfurt Anstand absolved them from fulfilling their part of the agreement. However, in contrast to the Catholics who also refused to help Ferdinand in protest against Hapsburg policies in Germany, the Schmalkaldians promised long-term assistance as soon as Charles' approval of the agreement was secured. Ferdinand promised to seek favorable action from Charles. At the same time, the Schmalkaldians supported the Catholic demands for prompt settlement of Germany's problems. Particularly they endorsed the request for concurrent settlement of religious and political problems at a Reichstag acting as a national council.

This action had far-reaching implications. It was taken on the assumption that Charles would oppose the meeting of any national council—so contrary to the imperial idea and desire for church reform—before all avenues to a general Christian council were closed. The Emperor was therefore expected to continue his efforts to persuade Paul III to reconvene the prorogued Council of Mantua. But the war of the Holy League in the Mediterranean, together with traditional papal opposition to a general council, seemed certain to delay any meeting well beyond the minimum time limits of the Frankfurt Anstand. Such considerations, the Protestants hoped, might induce Charles to recognize the Frankfurt agreement in order to gain enough time to arrange the meeting of a general council. However, should Charles accept the Catholic program for German pacification, they contemplated a compromise with the Catholics and the Emperor. In return for minor concessions in matters of faith they would seek official recognition or, depending on circumstances, perhaps even the expansion, of the gains secured at Frankfurt. In any event, support of the Catholic conciliar plan in the summer of 1539 was calculated to reduce Catholic opposition to the Frankfurt Anstand and encourage Charles to ratify the document. Finally, the Protestants tried to convince Charles directly of their desire to seek a peaceful and prompt solution of Germany's problems, of their willingness to support Ferdinand's plans in the East and of their loyalty to the Emperor and the King of the Romans. But none of the Protestant actions, nor the efforts of several emissaries, could persuade Charles to approve the Frankfurt agreement.

As the Schmalkaldians had feared, the Emperor found the agreement unsatisfactory.[26] He was displeased with the concessions made to the Lutherans and the provisions regarding German pacification. His first impulse was to reject the Anstand altogether. He would seek a truce with Constantinople that would release him to concentrate on the settlement of Germany's problems. He would intensify his efforts to reassemble the Council of Mantua as soon as possible and, in the interim, oppose, by force if necessary, any Protestant action deviating from the provisions of the Religious Peace of Nürnberg. The realities of the international situation forced a reconsideration of this plan. The Turkish fleet scored a major victory against the Holy League at Castelnuovo during the summer, and the Porte rejected Charles' truce overtures shortly thereafter. The Emperor therefore decided to concentrate on the very action that would make ratification of the Frankfurt Anstand unnecessary—the immediate summoning of a general council. But his efforts proved futile, for Paul III, encouraged by Francis, refused to follow the Emperor's lead. Despite these adverse conditions until the spring of 1540 Charles resisted the Protestant pressure for ratification of the Frankfurt agreement and Catholic demands for

[26] For Charles' reaction to the Frankfurt *Anstand* and his policies before April 18, 1540 consult Brandi, *Charles V*, 430 ff.; Fuchtel, *Der Frankfurter*, 201 ff.; A. Korte, *Die Konzilspolitik Karl V in den Jahren 1538–1543* (Halle a.d.S., 1905), 19 ff. Also *N. B.*, V, 192–198.

convening the national council. On April 18 of that year the Emperor reluctantly offered the Germans a compromise solution. He would agree to a summer meeting of Catholic and Protestant leaders to seek a preliminary accord on outstanding spiritual and secular differences. A definitive solution would be sought by the Emperor and Germany's estates at a later date.

Charles' proposition, made because of a gradual worsening of the international situation in the Mediterranean and Italy, was intentionally ambiguous. It would appease both Protestants and Catholics without committing him to ratification of the Frankfurt Anstand or to immediate summoning of a national council. The prolonged and inconclusive negotiations likely at the preliminary meeting should also work to his advantage. They should allow him sufficient time to counter the very factors that made it necessary to treat with the Germans at all. Charles would join the Venetians in seeking peace in the Mediterranean by negotiations with the Porte for a truce. If successful in this, he could concentrate on Italy and discourage the threatened renewal of hostilities by Suleiman's ally, Francis I. A show of strength in Milan, Piedmont, and Savoy might not only cause Francis to agree to a definitive peace in the West but force both him and the Pope to consent to an immediate meeting of the council. Charles' plans, however, came to naught and in January 1541 he summoned the national council he had hoped to forestall. The timing was related to a major crisis in Hungary.[27]

In the summer of 1540 John Zápolya died suddenly. However, despite the understanding of Grosswardein, Ferdinand did not become King of Hungary. Zápolya's followers, seeking to maintain Hungary's precarious independence, immediately proclaimed his infant son, John Sigismund, king. Suleiman's recognition of the new monarch was sought at once. Infuriated by this violation of the Treaty of Grosswardein, Ferdinand decided to force his claim. In the fall of 1540 he led an army against Buda, the Hungarian capital. He had already dispatched a special envoy, Hieronimus Laski, to Constantinople to secure Ottoman recognition of his

[27] On the Hungarian crisis consult documents in von Gevay, *Urkunden,* III³, 70 ff.

usurped rights. Neither of Ferdinand's measures succeeded. Suleiman, angered by the invasion of Hungary, imprisoned Laski and prepared for war in the spring. Meanwhile he ordered intensification of corsair activities in the Mediterranean. Charles' hopes for a truce with the Porte died and fears of another outbreak of general warfare in the West grew. Might not Francis resume hostilities under the circumstances? [28] According to the Hapsburg strategy devised in the early winter, Charles would maintain his forces in Italy and the Mediterranean and Ferdinand would seek assistance from Germany. Charles would support his brother to the extent of agreeing to the convocation of a national German council. Historic precedent and contemporary statements by Catholic and Protestant leaders indicated that such action was necessary to ensure support for Ferdinand against the Turks and perhaps even for the defense of the Empire.

Charles' summons of January 1541, though precipitated by the Turkish situation, nevertheless represented a sincere attempt to find a solution to Germany's problems.[29] The preliminary negotiations between Catholic and Protestant secular leaders and theologians, begun with Charles' consent in 1540, gave the Emperor reason to believe that a compromise settlement might be worked out at a national council. While no positive agreement had been reached at the political meeting of Hagenau, negotiations had been in progress on an outwardly friendly basis since June. An encouraging sign was the decision taken early during the meeting to permit concurrent discussions among theologians at Worms. The meeting of theologians which opened late in the fall also reflected an atmosphere of good will if not willingness to compromise immediately. The only element of general agreement at Hagenau and Worms was the announced determination to seek a solution to Germany's problems and accord this issue priority over any other.

Charles' reluctance to summon the national council was further diminished by apparent papal support for such a gathering. Paul

[28] On this point see Charrière, *Négociations,* I, 421 ff.
[29] For Charles' motivations see *N. B.,* V, 447 ff., VI, 35 ff.; also Korte, *Die Konzilspolitik,* 31–47.

III had indicated by word and deed that he would approve a satisfactory compromise of theological differences. His delegation at Worms, which included such dignitaries as Contarini and Campeggio, was to impress the Emperor by its presence and verbal assurances of the sincerity of the Pope. Under the circumstances, the imperial order of January 17, 1541, calling the Lutheran and Catholic estates and theologians to assemble at Regensburg on April 7 to seek a solution to Germany's political and religious difficulties and grant aid against the Turks was issued in a spirit of guarded optimism. It was received in the same spirit by Catholics and Protestants. All summoned, except the Elector of Saxony, agreed to meet on the appointed date.

But, as the Emperor was soon to discover, his hopefulness was unjustified. He learned, after April 7, that the aims of the Catholics and Protestants were irreconcilable and that the Protestants in particular would attempt to exploit the Hapsburg need for assistance against the Turks for their own ends.

As the Diet of Regensburg opened, the Emperor asked that pending the conclusion of the theological discussions, the estates consider the question of assistance against the Turks.[30] The Diet agreed to consider Charles' request, demanding, however, that immediate action be taken toward the settlement of Germany's political problems. The Emperor agreed, whereupon the Catholics and Protestants revealed their plans. The Catholics, obviously encouraged by Charles' presence in Germany and the deceptively conciliatory attitude displayed by the Schmalkaldians since 1539, demanded a permanent settlement on the basis of the Augsburg Recess of 1530. The Protestants, on the other hand, doubting the possibility of reconciliation

---

[30] The best general account on the Diet of Regensburg is by F. Roth, "Zur Geschichte des Reichstages zu Regensburg im Jahre 1541," *Archiv für Reformationsgeschichte,* 2 (1904–1905), 250–269, with excellent documentary material, *ibid.,* 270–307 and *ibid.,* 3 (1905–1906), 18–64. For Charles' policies at Regensburg consult P. Heidrich, *Karl V und die deutschen Protestanten am Vorabend des Schmalkaldischen Krieges* (Frankfurt a.M., 1911), I, 15 ff.; for the Protestant position *ibid.,* 17 ff., and *P. C.,* III, 178 ff. The documents contained in *N. B.,* VII, 5 ff., are especially valuable for appraising the policies of the Catholic forces at the Diet.

of theological differences, insisted on permanent, official, and unlimited recognition of Lutheranism and legal equality for all Germans regardless of faith. Disheartened by the rigidity of the conflicting views, the Emperor urged moderating on both sides. He would need time to study the plans carefully and, in any event, would delay action pending the outcome of the theological discussions. Meanwhile he would expect the Reichstag to commit itself on aid against the Turk. Charles' answer elicited no favorable response. The Diet would continue to consider his request for subsidies but no action would be taken until progress was made on German issues. Charles decided to temporize, hoping that a theological compromise which would lead to political compromise as well might be reached. By early June, however, the theological discussions appeared deadlocked, the basic Catholic and Lutheran positions remained unchanged, and no progress on the question of aid was reported. Charles suggested that both sides submit new plans for a temporary solution of Germany's problems and expedite action on subsidies against the Turks. Alarming reports from Constantinople on the imminence of the Ottoman offensive prompted the Emperor's plea. The Catholics refused to compromise with the Protestants but expressed their willingness to give urgent consideration to the request for aid. The Protestant leaders however, rejected both suggestions, warning the Emperor that no assistance would be granted unless he acceded to their demands for *Friede* and *Recht*.

Before Charles could formulate a policy to meet this situation, events in Hungary forced a revision of the Protestant terms. On June 25, Ferdinand, who had been absent fighting in Hungary, appeared before the Diet.[31] Reporting that the Turks had already left Constantinople, he implored the granting of instant assistance lest his forces be destroyed and the road to the Empire left open for the Infidel. Ferdinand's desperate appeal resulted in an immediate Catholic offer of 10,000 men and 3,000 horses for the defense of Hungary.

[31] The impact of Ferdinand's appeal is admirably evaluated by the papal nuncio Sanzio in *N. B.*, VII, 68–69. On this point see also *N. B.*, VII, 67 ff.

The Catholic response was not motivated entirely by sympathy for Ferdinand's plight; it was also designed to enhance Charles' position *vis-à-vis* the Protestants by reducing Hapsburg dependency on Lutheran assistance and by strengthening Ferdinand's military position in Hungary. Most Catholics expected to be rewarded at least by imperial support for their original plan. The Catholic League even recommended joint military action against the Protestants to enforce that plan. The Protestants, however, were more influenced by the Catholics' generosity to Ferdinand than was the Emperor. In the face of an imminent Turkish attack against Hungary and perhaps even the Empire itself, Charles favored a temporary compromise with the Lutherans on terms less drastic than the Catholic ones. He would contemplate military action only in the improbable event of Protestant insistence on permanent or long-term recognition and even then only under conditions more propitious than those of the summer of 1541. But the immovable Catholic stand toward the Lutherans was to affect Charles' negotiating tactics and the nature of his ultimate compromise with the Protestants.

The significance of the Catholic action could not escape the Schmalkaldians.[32] To offset it they promised equivalent aid against the Turks on July 3. Still, the price of their assistance would be the settlement of Germany's problems on the basis of *Friede* and *Recht*. *Friede,* however, was now interpreted as the right to undisturbed exercise and dissemination of their religion, *Recht* as the termination of Kammergericht action in matters of faith and the inclusion of Protestants in the Imperial Chamber. "Long term" also replaced "permanent" in their demand for recognition in Germany. The possibility of compromise was thus held out to the Emperor.

Charles delayed acceptance until July 12 when the theologians abandoned their efforts to reconcile conflicting dogma and the Turks were reported officially en route to Hungary. On July 19 he made his initial reply to the demands of the Protestants, offering them a political truce for six months. These terms appeared conservative,

---

[32] The documents in Roth, *Zur Geschichte,* 2, 276 ff., and 3, 23 ff., are essential for studying Protestant policies.

yet they reflected accurately the Emperor's position in mid-July. Charles needed the six months' respite to fend off the Turkish threat to Hungary and the Empire and to undertake further steps to stabilize the German situation. During this period he would make a last effort to persuade the Pope to convene a general Christian council under circumstances more favorable than those of the summer of 1541. The Protestants, however, rejected Charles' offer and restated their July 3 terms. The ensuing aggravation of the Turkish crisis soon broke the deadlock.

Ferdinand's appeals for assistance increased in direct proportion to the rapidity of the Turkish advance toward Hungary. They reach their zenith late in July when the Turks were reported within striking distance of southern Hungary. The members of the Reichstag were alarmed; some delegates even gave credence to a rumor that the Ottoman armies were intent on reaching Regensburg itself.[33] As under similar circumstances in the past the Lutheran estates were under mounting pressure to grant unconditional assistance for the defense of the Empire as were the Protestant leaders to modify their demands. Unknown to the Protestants, the Emperor too was under pressure to alter his stand. Late in July Charles received disturbing reports from Italy of a plot between Francis I and Suleiman.[34] Emissaries of the French monarch en route to Constantinople to coordinate a joint Franco-Turkish attack on the Hapsburgs had been captured and murdered by imperial agents. Fear of retaliatory action by the French, possibly in conjunction with the Turkish fleet, caused Charles to modify his plans. He would liberalize the terms of his offer to the Protestants and prepare for immediate action in the West. On July 26 he made a second counteroffer to the Schmalkaldian proposal of July 3.

Charles now proposed that the decision of the theologians, em-

---

[33] *N. B.,* VII, 76. On German fears, in general, Roth, *Zur Geschichte,* 3, 23 ff.; on those of the Lutheran estates specifically, *P. C.,* III, 201 ff. Among contemporary *Flugschriften* see the interesting *Anschlag wider die grawsamen und blutdürstigen Tyranney der Türcken* (n.p., 1541).

[34] This matter is discussed in detail by Ursu, *La Politique,* 107 ff., 118 ff.; documents in Charrière, *Négociations,* I, 423 ff., 474–488.

bodied in the Book of Regensburg, be presented to a general council for further consideration. A national council would undertake this task and renew its attempt to settle all German problems in case a general council could not be convoked within eighteen months. Pending enactment of either alternative, he would reconfirm the provisions of the Religious Peace of Nürnberg as emended by the Frankfurt Anstand, including suspension of Kammergericht action contrary to the spirit of those agreements. He would also issue guarantees of Catholic observance of these terms for a period not longer than eighteen months. All other provisions of the Augsburg Recess of 1530 not in conflict with these stipulations would, however, remain in force until final settlement of Germany's problems.

The Schmalkaldians sought to alter Charles' terms on the assumption that further concessions might be made as the Turks advanced on Hungary. They therefore requested removal of all limitations on expansion of their faith and appointment of Protestants to the Kammergericht. The Emperor would not agree to these demands. The Catholics had already protested against the terms of his offer of July 26 and he himself thought that he had probably been excessively generous to the Schmalkaldians. However, he decided to adopt an apparently conciliatory policy recommended by his close advisers, Cardinal de Granvelle and the Count of Naves. These trusted counselors urged Charles to issue further guarantees to the Protestants and later seek their revocation through conciliar, or if necessary even military action as soon as the international situation would permit. He should also secure Catholic consent for any agreement that would be reached with the Protestants by assuring them of his intention to revise it to their satisfaction as soon as feasible. Therefore, on July 29 Charles issued the Declaration of Regensburg which removed restrictions on the expansion of Lutheranism except through action that would "forcibly entice away or take under their [Lutheran] protection the subjects of any Catholic state." [35] It also removed the barriers to the appointment of Lutherans to the Imperial Chamber. The Declaration would supplement the Book of Regensburg and be conditional on Lutheran

[35] Von Döllinger, *Beiträge,* I, 36–38.

assistance to Ferdinand for the defense of Hungary and the Empire against the Turks. The Protestant leadership accepted Charles' terms. Men, horses, and supplies would be dispatched to Hungary immediately and the Lutheran estates would join the Catholic at Speyer in January 1542 to consider the question of permanent subsidies for defense against the Infidel.

However, at the end of July 1541, the Protestant leaders began to realize that no decisive victory had been gained at Regensburg and that the Emperor would soon seek to repudiate the concessions he had granted under duress.[36] Charles' readiness to agree to the terms he had so steadfastly opposed in the past, his hasty departure for Italy on July 31 and, above all, the willingness of the Catholic estates to incorporate the main provisions of the Book and Declaration into the Recess of the Diet aroused the suspicion of even the most conservative members of the Protestant camp. But they also understood that time was on their side. The possibility of Charles' attaining his goals in the West within eighteen months appeared remote. The belligerent activities of Francis and the Turkish fleet virtually precluded peace or even a stable truce in the foreseeable future. Papal consent to a general council seemed equally unlikely. The apparent insolubility of the Hungarian crisis was particularly reassuring. The Protestants expected an aggravation of the conflict between Hapsburg and Turk unless Ferdinand should abandon his claims to Hungary. This possibility was, however, eliminated by events in the summer of 1541. Consequently, they would make use of whatever opportunities might develop from Charles' involvement in the West and Ferdinand's in the East to consolidate the gains of Regensburg and strive to obtain Hapsburg and Catholic consent for long-term, if not permanent adoption of their program of *Friede* and *Recht*. The first major opportunity came in January 1542 at Speyer. It resulted, as anticipated, from Ottoman action in Hungary.

The Turkish attack on Hungary had reached its height in August 1541. A German army, quickly assembled at the close of the

---

[36] An excellent discussion of the Lutheran position may be found in Heidrich, *Karl V*, 50 ff.

Regensburg Diet, was virtually destroyed by the Turks. By August 26 Buda and Pest had fallen. On August 28 the Sultan agreed to recognize Zápolya's son as King of Hungary upon his coming of age, and would act as regent himself in the meantime. The Hungarian region between the Danube and the Theiss (the so-called Territory of Ofen) would be placed under direct Turkish control to fortify the country's defenses against possible attack by Ferdinand. The Turks returned to Constantinople in September without attempting a direct attack against the Empire or Ferdinand's forces west of Buda.

Suleiman's action roused to panic the Hungarian nobility who now generally favored implementation of the Treaty of Grosswardein, at least to the extent of empowering Ferdinand to act as regent for young John Sigismund.[37] The King of the Romans intended military intervention at his earliest opportunity. He appeared confident that the Territory of Ofen could be freed from Turkish domination, since the Ottoman forces guarding it were few and virtually no opposition was anticipated from the Hungarians. However, to stage a successful counteroffensive and afterward to defend Hungary against certain Turkish retaliation he needed men, materiel, and a guarantee of long-range assistance from Germany. Provision had been made at Regensburg for just such a contingency. Therefore, in October he formally convened the Catholic and Protestant estates to Speyer on January 14, 1542 to consider the question of permanent subsidies.

The Schmalkaldians immediately assembled at Naumburg to formulate a specific policy for the Speyer meeting.[38] They noted

[37] The impact of Ottoman action in Hungary is admirably treated by F. Salamon, *Ungarn im Zeitalter der Türkenherrschaft* (Leipzig, 1887), 82 ff. Ferdinand's reaction is discussed in detail by von Bucholtz, *Geschichte,* V, 160 ff.

[38] On Protestant policies consult H. Traut, *Kurfürst Joachim II von Brandenburg und der Türkenfeldzug vom Jahre 1542* (Gummersbach, 1892), 11 ff.; Mentz, *Johann Friedrich,* III, 302 ff. See also Johann Frederick of Saxony and Philip of Hesse to Maurice of Saxony, October 24, 1541 in E. Brandenburg, ed., *Politische Korrespondenz des Herzogs und Kurfürsten Moritz von Sachsen* (Leipzig, 1900), I, 224–225; Maurice of Saxony to his delegates at

with satisfaction that Charles was engaged in battle with the Turks at Algiers and that Ferdinand was anxious to secure subsidies as soon as possible. However, they also took cognizance of the Germans' increased willingness to support Ferdinand in Hungary, now that part of that Christian country had been annexed by the Infidel. This attitude was certain to influence the Lutheran delegates at Speyer and thus limit the concessions that could be exacted from the King of the Romans. It would also affect the Catholics who might exceed earlier commitments and thereby further reduce the Schmalkaldians' bargaining power. Hence, the Protestant leaders decided to demand long-term recognition for the Lutheran faith and immediate appointment of Protestants to the Kammergericht and settle for whatever satisfactory compromise could be concluded.

The Schmalkaldian plan was successfully implemented at Speyer.[39] After the King of the Romans rejected their initial demands, the Schmalkaldians agreed to accept his compromise offer which would extend the Regensburg guarantees for five years and open the Kammergericht to Lutherans in the immediate future. The Protestants would join the Catholics in raising an army to free the Territory of Ofen from the Infidel and bring all of Hungary into the Hapsburg fold. The German forces would assemble in Vienna and be ready for action in May 1542.

The alacrity with which Ferdinand offered terms so acceptable to the Protestants and the subsequent approval of the compromise by the Catholics and Charles caused a revision of Schmalkaldian strategy.[40] The Protestant leaders suspected collusion between the King of the Romans and the Catholics when the latter consented to incorporate the new concessions into the Recess. It seemed evident that

---

Speyer, January 6, 1542 and January 25, 1542, *ibid.,* I, 299–300, 319; Maurice of Saxony to Philip of Hesse, February 19, 1542, *ibid.,* I, 335–336; Jean de Naves to Charles, November 12, 1541, Lanz, *Correspondenz,* II, 330; Philip of Hesse to the Rat of Strassburg, November 18, 1541, *P. C.,* III, 216–217.

[39] The best account of the negotiations at Speyer may be found in Heidrich, *Karl V,* I, 60 ff.

[40] For Protestant policies after Speyer consult Traut, *Kurfürst,* 47 ff. and Heidrich, *Karl V,* I, 72 ff., 84 ff.

Ferdinand had agreed to a Catholic plan to repudiate the new guarantees as soon as practicable, by military action if necessary. Charles' acceptance of the Recess, initially opposed by the Count of Naves, his representative at Speyer, convinced them that the Emperor too had become a party to the scheme. The Protestant high command therefore decided that their best defense would be to take the initiative from their enemies. They would, of course, continue to press their campaign for legal recognition as opportunities arose; however, they would strengthen their strategic position in Germany through territorial aggrandizement by force. Comparatively little risk would be involved as such action would be undertaken only when the Hapsburgs and Catholics could not strike back, and must accept the *fait accompli*. The spring of 1542 appeared highly propitious for an initial military coup. Charles had been defeated in his attempt to conquer Algiers and was rebuilding his forces for the imminent renewal of war with Francis. Ferdinand was ready to lead an expedition into Hungary. Catholics as well as Lutherans would be involved in this conflict. Convinced that no counteraction was feasible under such circumstances, the Schmalkaldians decided to annex the Duchy of Brunswick.

The revised Schmalkaldian policy put into practice in 1542 was an extremely hazardous one. More than any other factor it contributed to the outbreak of the Schmalkaldian War. Actually, the strategy was based on several erroneous assumptions. In 1542 the Catholics alone considered war the only effective method of arresting the growth of Lutheranism and enforcing the provisions of the Recess of Augsburg.[41] Ferdinand, on the contrary, desired a peaceful solution of Germany's problems.[42] The standing Turkish threat to Hungary and his dependence on German assistance to combat it made peace imperative. At Speyer, the King of the Romans advised the Catholic leaders that he favored revocation of the new guarantees as soon as possible. He assumed that this would be achieved either by a general or a national council. Only as a last

---

[41] Janssen, *History*, VI, 195 ff.
[42] For details on Ferdinand's position consult von Bucholtz, *Geschichte*, IV, 388 ff.

resort would he participate in a war against the Protestants. The subsequent Catholic actions at Speyer which misled the Schmalkaldians regarding Ferdinand's ultimate intentions were prompted by different motivations than those attributed to them by the Protestants. They were actually designed to force the Emperor to take action. Surely Charles would not countenance Lutheran enjoyment of such extravagant concessions for too long. The Catholics apparently excluded the possibility that the concessions could be revoked by conciliar action alone and expected Charles to join them in fighting the Protestants when conditions would permit. The Schmalkaldians also envisaged this possibility which, of course, caused them greater concern than speculations of collusion between Ferdinand and the Catholics. They too regarded Charles' acceptance of the Speyer Recess as a prelude to eventual repudiation by military means. But in the spring of 1542, both Protestants and Catholics were mistaken in their appraisal of the Emperor's future intentions.

In 1542 Charles knew that too many concessions had been made to the Lutherans under duress and he emphatically intended to invalidate at least those conflicting with the provisions of the Religious Peace of Nürnberg of 1532 as soon as he could.[43] Nevertheless, he still preferred conciliar to military methods. The unstable international situation in both West and East virtually precluded his going to war with the Protestants in the foreseeable future. Only in the event of the Schmalkaldians' rejecting the decisions of any council or taking military action against the Hapsburgs and the Catholics of the Empire would Charles resort to war as the means of settling Germany's problems. Schmalkaldian action in Brunswick, however, forced Charles to support the Catholic solution.

A detailed account of the preliminaries to the Schmalkaldian War

[43] Charles' position may be appraised by consulting the documents contained in "Aktenstücke zur Politik Kaiser Karl V im Herbst 1541," W. Friedensburg, ed., *Archiv für Reformationsgeschichte*, 29 (1932), 35 ff., as well as his correspondence in Lanz, *Correspondenz*, II, 328 ff. See also Brandi, *Charles V*, 467 ff.

would be beyond the scope of this study. Nor is it necessary to consider in detail the intrinsic motivations and diplomacy of the main contenders in the conflict, the Catholics, the Protestants, and the Hapsburgs. Their actions and decisions were generally motivated by factors not directly related to Ottoman problems. The role of the Turks in the prelude to the war of 1546–1547 was nevertheless significant as their very quiescence after 1543 permitted Charles and Ferdinand to join the Catholics in warring against the League of Schmalkalden.

In the spring of 1542, as their men joined the Catholic troops and those of Ferdinand at Vienna, the Schmalkaldians were preparing the attack on the Duchy of Brunswick.[44] The coup was staged in the summer of 1542, when the war between Charles and Francis had just been resumed and Ferdinand was leading into Hungary an army which included the forces of Henry of Brunswick. It seemed that there could be no military reprisal, but the Catholics promptly initiated Kammergericht action against the Schmalkaldians and enforcement of the judicial decision was threatened by the Catholic League. The Schmalkaldians challenged the jurisdiction of the Imperial Chamber, from which they claimed to be exempted under the Speyer guarantees. The Catholics thereupon requested Ferdinand to repudiate these guarantees to legalize their contemplated counteraction. Ferdinand refused on the grounds that his involvement in Hungary and Charles' war with Francis made any move that might lead to war in Germany too dangerous.[45]

Ferdinand's position was determined by developments affecting Hapsburg interests in both the East and the West. The renewal of war between Charles and the French monarch anticipated resumption of the Turkish offensive against Hungary and the Empire.

---

[44] Detailed accounts of the events of 1542–1543 may be found in Janssen, *History*, VII, 195 ff., and von Ranke, *Deutsche Geschichte*, IV, 214 ff.

[45] For Ferdinand's position consult *N. B.*, VII, 262 ff.; also von Bucholtz, *Geschichte*, V, 167 ff.

Francis had indeed asked his ally Suleiman to create a diversion in the East in 1543. To upset Francis' plans, Charles had requested Ferdinand to secure support from Germany sufficient to discourage any major Turkish offensive. If this worked, the men and supplies could then be used against the French. Charles' plan was based on the premise that Turks would not be able to stage a major offensive on such short notice, particularly after their undistinguished Hungarian campaign of 1541. Ferdinand agreed with the Emperor on the need to raise men and materiel but was less sanguine than his brother as to the Ottoman war potential. He too doubted the likelihood of a Turkish attack against the Empire but feared that the defenses of the Territory of Ofen would be strengthened beyond hope of reconquest unless substantial assistance for exclusive use in Hungary could be quickly secured. Ferdinand's pessimism resulted from the abortive expedition of 1542 when the German army failed to breach the fortifications of the Territory of Ofen in spite of the numerical weakness of the enemy. The ignominious withdrawal of the German forces from Buda in November after a futile siege convinced the King of the Romans that his plans could be realized only if disciplined and well-equipped armies were to exert constant pressure on the Turks. Only then could he expect the Hungarians to side with him against the Ottoman regent and the infant king. In any event, in the winter 1542–1543 the Hapsburg interests were too closely linked to German harmony and assistance to risk any action which might precipitate war between the Catholic and Schmalkaldian leagues.

However, repeating the tactics used in 1542, the King of the Romans reassured the Catholics as to his determination to repudiate the guarantees of Speyer as soon as circumstances would allow. In the interim, to bring that moment closer, he would expect the Catholics to continue their policy of providing him assistance for Hungary. Formal action would be taken at a Diet where he would also seek Lutheran support by temporarily reconfirming the guarantees of Speyer. The Catholics agreed reluctantly. In February 1543 they joined with the Lutheran estates at Nürnberg to grant aid for the defense of Hungary and the Empire against the anticipated Turkish offensive.[46]

At Nürnberg the King of the Romans was presented with impossible demands by the Protestants. By February 1543, the Schmalkaldians had agreed upon the necessity of ironclad guarantees that the provisions of the recesses of Regensburg and Speyer would not be repudiated. Catholic actions following the seizure of Brunswick, moreover, had convinced them that only formal suspension of all Kammergericht proceedings would give them immunity from legal and military reprisals. They therefore requested reconfirmation of the Speyer guarantees, broadened to include suspension of the activities of the Imperial Chamber until 1547. The Schmalkaldian demands were rejected by Ferdinand shortly after the opening of the Diet. He was prepared to renew the guarantees of Speyer *pro forma,* even for ten years, but could not take any radical action affecting the Kammergericht. The maximum concession he would make was to suspend pending Kammergericht proceedings in the Brunswick case and seek Catholic approval for this step. The Schmalkaldians would have accepted this offer, if carried out, but the Catholics refused *de jure* recognition of the seizure of Brunswick. To prevent Ferdinand from concluding a unilateral agreement with the Schmalkaldians if enticed by the bait of substantial aid against the Turks, the Catholic estates seized the initiative in this respect. Late in March they granted assistance consisting of 24,000 men and 4,000 horses, conditional on Ferdinand's withdrawing his tentative offer to the Protestants. This step was decisive in directing Ferdinand's course.

Faced with Catholic obstruction of an indispensable guarantee, the Schmalkaldians advised Ferdinand that no assistance could be expected unless he secured Catholic approval for his terms. The King of the Romans tried to persuade the Catholics to alter their resolution but his task became hopeless as the Turkish threat dwindled during April. By the end of the month it became ap-

[46] Details on the negotiations at Nürnberg may be found in *N. B.,* VII, 307 ff.; *P. C.,* III, 347 ff. Heidrich, *Karl V,* I, 117 ff., and Mentz, *Johann Friedrich,* III, 501 ff. are particularly valuable for studying Schmalkaldian policies.

parent to all assembled at Nürnberg that a major Ottoman offensive would not occur in 1543. Only minor troop movements, precursors of limited action in Hungary, were reported. Under the circumstances, the Catholics remained obdurate in their determination not to compromise. The waning of the Turkish threat also strengthened the Schmalkaldian position. The Protestant leaders, fearing a possible diversion of the forces recruited for Hungary against the Lutherans, insisted on acceptance of their terms. However, to lure Ferdinand away from the Catholics and encourage action in Hungary, they conditionally offered to match the assistance granted by the Catholic estates. But Ferdinand, regardless of his personal interests in Hungary, could not accede to a request so adamantly opposed by the Catholics. Therefore, he adjourned the Diet of Nürnberg with the deepened conviction that reconciliation of Catholic and Protestant interests had become virtually impossible after the Brunswick coup. However, he still would not become a party to a military showdown with the Protestants as long as the war continued in the West and the Hungarian situation remained unsettled.

The feeling that war was nearer also prevailed among the Schmalkaldians. The likelihood of attack by the Catholics and Ferdinand in 1543 was generally discounted because of Charles' involvement in the West but preparations to protect Protestant gains by legal means and by force, if necessary, would be accelerated. While Schmalkaldian tactics would change in detail between 1543 and 1546, their constant basic aim was to immobilize the opposition and secure reconfirmation of the terms of Regensburg and Speyer whenever possible. Their main target was, of course, Charles—the principal power to be reckoned with in war or peace. The Schmalkaldians would work to prolong his war against Francis and encourage action against the Turks in order to divert his attention from German affairs. They would placate him by offering their assistance toward the achievement of Hapsburg goals in Europe and limiting their demands for legal recognition until the danger of war against the Lutherans themselves should have been averted. However, Charles could not be sufficiently appeased, and the Schmalkaldian plan failed.

After the Brunswick coup, Charles decided to restore religious uniformity and peace in Germany by conciliar action or war.[47] As either of these alternatives depended on victory in the West and peace in the East, the Emperor formulated a policy designed to achieve these prerequisities as soon as possible. The essentials of the new plan were revealed in the summer of 1543 when Charles arrived in Germany to organize a major campaign against Francis' ally, the Duke of Cleves. He wished to secure German assistance to hasten his triumph over Francis' forces. In order to obtain subsidies he planned to assure the Catholics of his decision to repudiate all concessions made the Lutherans in the past, while the Protestants of his willingness to reconfirm the guarantees of Speyer. At the same time he would *sub rosa* persuade Ferdinand to seek a truce with Constantinople until the French and German problems were settled and joint Hapsburg action could be undertaken against Suleiman. He would request assistance against the French and the Turk but actually use the subsidies against Francis and deceive the Protestants as to his true intentions toward the Porte. Charles' policy was a successful one.

When a new Reichstag assembled on the Emperor's orders at Speyer in February 1544, Catholics and Lutherans agreed to grant subsidies against Francis and the Turks.[48] The Catholic action was based on the knowledge that Charles would turn to German affairs once victory over Francis was achieved; the Protestants agreed due to the mistaken assumption that the Emperor would be unable to realize the military and political aims announced at the Diet. Charles had asked the estates to assist him in his war against the French king and the Turkish fleet in the Mediterranean. Upon completion of military campaigns against these enemies he would lead an

[47] For Charles' policies before the Diet of Speyer see Brandi, *Charles V*, 467 ff., 501 ff.; Heidrich, *Karl V*, II, 7 ff.; also Lanz, *Staatspapiere*, 380 ff.
[48] The best general account of the Diet of Speyer is by A. de Boor, *Beiträge zur Geschichte des Speirer Reichstages vom Jahre 1544* (Strassburg, 1878), 3 ff. For Charles' policies see also Weiss, *Papiers*, III, 638 ff., and A. von Druffel, *Kaiser Karl V und die Römische Curie 1544–46* (München, 1877), I, 107 ff.

offensive against the Ottoman Empire. Only when victory had been achieved would he seek a permanent solution for the problems of the Empire at a general Christian council. He expressed high hopes for the realization of all these goals. Francis' strategic position had been weakened by Charles' decisive victory over the Duke of Cleves. The military power of the Turks was apparently declining. Their fleet, while still active in the Mediterranean, had failed to provide the relief necessary for the French king; likewise, Suleiman had been unable to create a successful diversion in Hungary. The Sultan's brief and ineffectual Hungarian expedition of the summer of 1543 was the best evidence of Ottoman weakness and the strongest justification for prompt military action against the Porte. Finally, the Emperor could point to the Pope's encouraging attempt to reform the Church. The formation of the Society of Jesus in 1542 and Paul's avowed willingness to summon a general council as soon as peace was restored in Europe augured a speedy settlement of Germany's religious problems.

The Schmalkaldians, however, questioned Charles' optimistic prognosis.[49] They appeared confident of Francis' ability to defend himself successfully and his determination to resist the temptation of arranging a truce. Similarly, they expected Barbarossa to continue his raids regardless of any temporary defeats administered by Charles' fleet. Under these circumstances, the threatened meeting of a general council was unlikely in the near future. They were skeptical of Charles' sincerity in promising a crusade against the Ottoman Empire, but gained reassurance from the belief that Ferdinand would exploit Ottoman weakness to promote his claims to Hungary. If aid were granted specifically for action against the Turk, the King of the Romans would doubtless use it to further his own aims in the East. These considerations made the Schmalkaldians decide to support Charles in accordance with the League's policy of encouraging Hapsburg involvement in Europe in order to forestall either a council meeting or an armed conflict in Germany. The Emperor's willingness to reconfirm the decisions of

[49] Protestant tactics are carefully discussed by de Boor, *ibid.*, 26 ff., and Heidrich, *Karl V*, II, 17 ff. See also *P. C.*, III, 570 ff.

Regensburg and Speyer and to assure the estates that any aid granted would be used against both the French and the Turks added to the Protestant impression that they had resolved a major dilemma to their partisan advantage.

The Schmalkaldians realized, of course, that there were dangers involved in assisting the Emperor. Their aid might contribute to the eventual defeat of a potential ally—Francis I. It could also be used to strengthen the very Hapsburg and Catholic forces that might be turned against the Schmalkaldian League itself. They were also aware that the Pope might convene the general council under circumstances auspicious for the Roman Church. In February 1544, however, these possibilities all seemed remote.

Ensuing events demonstrated that the Schmalkaldians had miscalculated the risks inherent in their policy. In the fall of 1544, Charles concluded the compromise Peace of Crespy with Francis. The Pope immediately convened the Council of Trent for March 1545. In the spring of 1545 Charles and Ferdinand sent representatives to Constantinople to seek a truce with the Porte on the basis of *uti possedetis.* Suleiman, anxious to resume his war against Thamasp, welcomed the Hapsburg terms. An agreement, preliminary to a treaty of "permanent peace," was concluded in November, and the stage was set for the Schmalkaldian War. In the summer of 1546, when a conciliar solution of Germany's problems appeared doomed because of Protestant rejection of the authority and composition of the Council of Trent, the Emperor and the King of the Romans joined the Catholic League in the other alternative—war.[50]

From the conclusion of the Religious Peace of Nürnberg to the eve of the Schmalkaldian War, the Protestants had pursued a policy aimed at removing all obstacles to the legal consolidation and expansion of Lutheranism in Germany. By 1546, they had made substantial gains toward the realization of this goal, chiefly by exploiting opportunities arising from the conflict between the Hapsburgs and the Ottoman Turks. All formal acts reconfirming the Religious

[50] For a general discussion of the preliminaries to the Schmalkaldian War see Brandi, *Deutsche Geschichte,* 264 ff.; Janssen, *History,* VI, 285 ff.; von Ranke, *Deutsche Geschichte,* IV, 271 ff.

Peace of Nürnberg or sanctioning Lutheran expansion since 1532, with the possible exception of the Recess of Speyer of 1544 were clearly influenced by Turkish pressure in Hungary and the Mediterranean. In 1534, at Cadan, Ferdinand legitimized Hesse's coup in Würtemberg and reconfirmed the Religious Peace of Nürnberg in return for Schmalkaldian assurances of loyalty and subsidies in Hungary. Charles, involved with the Ottoman fleet, confirmed Ferdinand's action. In 1539 at Frankfurt, Ferdinand recognized Lutheran expansion since 1532 and agreed to temporary suspension of Kammergericht action objectionable to the Protestants, in order to protect his secular interests in Hungary against the Turks. In 1541, the Emperor himself under the stress of Turkish action in Hungary and the Mediterranean confirmed and extended the provisions of the Frankfurt Anstand. In 1543, at Speyer, the King of the Romans agreed to renew the provisions of the Regensburg Recess for a period of five years to secure peace in Germany and assistance against the Turks in Hungary. Finally, in 1544, at Nürnberg, Charles reconfirmed the Recesses of Regensburg and Speyer to secure aid against France and, allegedly, the Infidel Turk.

Although the legal concessions that the Schmalkaldians wrung from the Hapsburgs (and also the Catholics after 1541) were technically revokable by a general or national council, their magnitude was gradually appreciated by all groups. The Schmalkaldians understood after 1539 that permanent legal recognition could not be obtained merely by exploiting crises resulting from the European policies of the Hapsburgs and their consequent need for peace in Germany and subsidies against the Turk. Nevertheless, they persisted in a policy of securing as many legal concessions and guarantees as possible although it was known that they were not given in good faith after 1541. For these guarantees and concessions sanctioned and facilitated expansion up to 1542 and, after the Brunswick coup, gave the Schmalkaldians a respite during which they could consolidate their position in the Empire.

The Hapsburgs and Catholics, however, were not blind to the Protestant advances. The Catholics by 1532, Charles by 1541, and Ferdinand by 1543 saw that, despite the piecemeal and revokable nature of the concessions that had been made to the Lutherans in the past, their acquired rights and powers gravely threatened Hapsburg and Catholic interests and security. This realization, borne out by the events of 1542 and by Protestant rejection of a possible conciliar solution in 1545, caused the Emperor and Ferdinand to join the Catholics in the Schmalkaldian War in 1546. But 1546 was too late. The Hapsburg concessions to the Lutherans could no longer be countermanded.

Chapter V

The Results of Hapsburg Policy

During the Schmalkaldian War and for several years thereafter the Turks virtually ceased their hostilities against the Hapsburgs.[1] In the West action was limited to infrequent minor naval raids into the eastern Mediterranean. None was sufficiently serious to provoke organized retaliation or break the truce of 1545 during Charles' lifetime. In the East peace prevailed throughout the five-year truce concluded between Ferdinand and the Porte in 1547. War would be renewed only in 1552 over the unresolved problem of Hapsburg succession to the Hungarian throne.

Europe's respite from Turkish alarums was due to a shift in Ottoman foreign policy. Released from his commitment to Francis after the Treaty of Crespy and satisfied that Hapsburg involvement in the Schmalkaldian War and German affairs would prevent violation of his agreement with Charles and Ferdinand, the Sultan decided to concentrate on domestic problems. First, however, he wanted to restore Ottoman prestige in the Middle East. Financial difficulties resulting from unusually large military expenditures and loss of revenue from the interrupted Mediterranean trade forced a temporary retrenchment. So did the restlessness infecting the war-weary Janissaries and Spahis. Only essential expeditions would be undertaken henceforth. War against Shah Thamasp, whose surreptitious activities had been undermining the security of the Otto-

[1] The most elaborate account of Ottoman policies and the problems of the Ottoman Empire after 1547 is by von Hammer, *Histoire,* V, 595 ff., VI, 1 ff. A modern interpretation of Ottoman problems may be found in Jorga, *Geschichte,* III, 96 ff.

man Empire in Asia since 1539, was included in this category. But
as soon as a precarious victory has been won after a brief campaign
in 1548, Suleiman devoted his attention to rebuilding the state
finances and the morale of his troops. The process was still uncom-
pleted at the time Hungarian hostilities were resumed, in 1552.

The Ottoman preoccupation with internal matters had had its
impact on German affairs during the years immediately following
the Schmalkaldian War, particularly by withdrawing the "Turkish
threat"—the Protestants' chief lever for securing legal recognition.
The renewal of activity, however, would hasten the attainment of
that long-range goal by affecting developments that had arisen
independently between 1547 and 1552.

The legal status and future of Lutheranism were still undetermined in 1552, for neither the Schmalkaldian War nor imperial
measures taken subsequently had resolved Germany's problems.
Charles had intended to destroy the Schmalkaldian League and
thus force Lutheran attendance at Trent, but the war did not bring
about the desired results.[2] A major military victory had been registered by the Emperor and his allies in 1547. The Schmalkaldian
forces had been decisively defeated and their leaders surrendered
unconditionally. Some, including the Landgrave of Hesse and the
Elector of Saxony, had even been imprisoned on Charles' orders.
But reconciliation of the opposing faiths by conciliar action was not
achieved (nor even attempted) because the papacy was unwilling
to create conditions conducive to possible compromise. Paul III
showed no inclination to undertake the major reform of the Catholic
Church expected by the Emperor and the optimistic among German
Lutherans and Catholics. The papacy, rejecting compromise, would
keep reform strictly within the conservative, historic Catholic tradition. Imperial pressure failed to move the intransigent Pope.
Thereupon Charles, to force positive action at Trent, decided to

[2] On the Schmalkaldian War and its immediate consequences in Germany
consult Janssen, *History*, VI, 362 ff.; W. Maurenbrecher, *Karl V und die
deutschen Protestanten 1545–1555* (Düsseldorf, 1865), 141 ff.; F. Hartung,
Karl V und die deutschen Reichstände von 1546 bis 1555 (Halle a.S., 1910),
19 ff.

formulate his own terms for temporary reconciliation of doctrinal differences and settlement of Germany's political problems. Charles' solution was presented to the first postwar Reichstag at Augsburg in the spring of 1548.[3] It consisted of an unsatisfactory religious and political compromise. The theological provisions embodied in the Augsburg Interim of May 15, 1548 were based on doctrinal principles unacceptable either to theologians or worshippers. The political provisions, which deprived the Lutherans of all legal guarantees but recognized the *status quo de facto,* were opposed by Catholics and Lutherans alike. Charles' contention that this was merely an interim solution pending ratification or modification of the religious compromise by an enlarged Council of Trent failed to satisfy the victorious Catholics. The loss of all previous gains, their undetermined legal status, and the imprisonment of their leaders further embittered the defeated Lutherans. But the Augsburg Interim settlement was reluctantly accepted by all except a handful of Protestant princes who wished to resume the fight for permanent legal recognition of Lutheranism in Germany. The changed international and German conditions demanded the use of new tactics for the attainment of their goal.

In 1548, the Lutheran princes, headed by Albert Alcibiades of Brandenburg-Culmbach, decided that the most effective course of action would be the rebuilding of Hapsburg dependence on Protestant loyalty and support.[4] As a renewal of hostilities could not be looked for in Hungary because of Ottoman involvement in the Middle East and Ferdinand's acceptance of the *status quo* of 1547, the Lutherans cautiously turned toward France. Henry II, who succeeded his father in 1547, had approached them in 1548, suggesting an alliance against the Emperor. The Protestants hesitated

---

[3] On the Diet of Augsburg and the Interim see G. Wolf, "Der Augsburger Interim," *Deutsche Zeitschrift für Geschichtswissenschaft,* Neue Folge, II, Vierteljahrschrift I (Leipzig, 1897-98), 47 ff.; Maurenbrecher, *Karl V,* 183 ff.; Brandi, *Charles V,* 557 ff.; also Schmauss, *Neue Sammlung,* I[2], 527–609.

[4] A general discussion of Protestant reaction to the decisions of 1548 may be found in Maurenbrecher, *Karl V,* 250 ff. For Franco-Protestant relations consult Charrière, *Négociations,* II, 30 ff.

to enter upon a formal agreement as they feared Charles' superior military strength, but discussions continued between the French monarch and a gradually expanding Protestant group. Only in 1551 did the Lutherans, now led by Maurice of Saxony, conclude a secret alliance with Henry. At Lochau, in October, the Protestant conspirators and the French king agreed to launch a surprise attack against the Emperor in the spring of 1552. The timing of the agreement and subsequent military action had been carefully chosen by the Germans.

Several developments occurring in 1551 influenced the Protestant decision to challenge the Emperor by force. Perhaps the most significant was Charles' insistence on Lutheran attendance at a "free" Council of Trent. The Emperor appeared convinced, in the early spring of 1551, that Pope Julius III, Paul's successor, would accept the Interim as the basis of a general solution of the religious differences dividing the Western Church. Julius' promises of moderation, culminating in the reconvening of the adjourned council to Trent on May 1, 1551 coincided with the issuance of more urgent imperial demands for German participation. The specter of a dictated reconciliation and subsequent enforcement of the conciliar decision in Germany buttressed Lutheran determination to oppose such actions by military force. Nevertheless, certain factors still worked against the conclusion of an alliance with Henry II. The Emperor's forces in Germany were powerful enough to retaliate effectively and the French king himself seemed unprepared for effective warfare in the West. The situation was apparently unfavorable in the spring; however, it changed markedly during the summer and fall.

Ferdinand, who had unwillingly but patiently submitted to Charles' demands for nonintervention in Hungarian affairs pending settlement of Germany's problems, defied his brother's wishes in June.[5] The rift with Charles occurred over the question of succession to the Holy Roman Empire. The formula evolved by the

[5] Ferdinand's policies after 1547 may be appraised best through a study of the pertinent documents in von Bucholtz, *Geschichte,* IX, 726 ff., and in A. von Druffel, ed., *Beiträge zur Reichsgeschichte, 1546–1555* (München, 1873–1896), I, 501 ff.

Emperor in March 1551 provided that Philip of Spain succeed Ferdinand as King of the Romans upon Charles' death. Ferdinand was gravely disappointed as he had hoped that his own son, Maximilian, would eventually succeed him as Holy Roman Emperor instead of the unpopular Philip. The only concession he could wring from Charles was an agreement that Philip's candidacy should not be pressed should it seem to jeopardize Hapsburg succession altogether. Ferdinand considered this stipulation gave him sufficient latitude to permit him to create conditions that would obviate Philip's candidacy. Specifically, he contemplated uniting the eastern possessions of the Hapsburgs and Germany to form a political entity entirely separate from the family holdings in the West. The eastern Empire would eventually revert to Maximilian independently of the West European and overseas domains. Such a consolidation would require settlement of the Hungarian and German problems and elimination of Charles' domination over German affairs.

The initial step toward the attainment of these goals was directed toward Hungary.[6] Ottoman inactivity would be exploited to renegotiate the Treaty of Grosswardein with Zápolya's widow, Isabella, and her entourage. Discussions initiated in June were completed in July; the outcome exceeded Ferdinand's highest expectations. Isabella and the Hungarian nobility agreed that in view of present Ottoman weakness, Ferdinand would be preferable to Suleiman as ruler of their country. By the formal Agreement of Weissenburg of July 1551, they consented to the replacement of John Sigismund as King by Ferdinand in return for cash, lands, and protection against the expected Ottoman reprisals.

The news of the Weissenburg accord encouraged the Protestant conspirators.[7] The probable Turkish offensive in Hungary, they thought, would immobilize Ferdinand in the event of a Lutheran military coup directed against the Emperor. Therefore, negotiations

---

[6] Details on Ferdinand's Hungarian policies may be found in A. Huber, "Die Verhandlungen Ferdinands I mit Isabella von Siebenbürgen, 1551–1555," *Archiv für österreichische Geschichte*, LXXVIII (1892), 4 ff.

[7] For the impact of the Treaty of Weissenburg on the Protestants consult *P. C.*, IV¹, 1003 ff., V, 107 ff.

with Henry II were intensified in the late summer. However, it was Charles' uncompromising attitude on the settlement of German affairs that ultimately crystallized the Protestants' determination to sign the Treaty of Lochau. For the Emperor, ignoring the German opposition to his Interim and the unwillingness of the Council of Trent to carry out his plans for Church reform, announced that the imperial edict of 1548 should remain in force until Julius III and the Council acceded to his wishes. Charles' obduracy dissolved all Protestant hesitation. In October the conspirators decided that only surprise military action taken under optimum conditions could give Lutheranism legal status in Germany. Henry's direct cooperation and indirect assistance from Suleiman through his spring campaign in Hungary should ensure victory. In the spring of 1552 the Lutheran expectations were fulfilled. Henry was awaiting the outbreak of the conspiracy to attack Charles in the West and Suleiman had ordered a resumption of hostilities in Hungary to challenge the Weissenburg agreement. Maurice of Saxony and his associates therefore began the rebellion against the Emperor in March.

The uprising took Charles by surprise. He immediately withdrew to Innsbruck to rally his forces against the Protestants and the French who had invaded the Empire. To gain time he requested Ferdinand in April to ascertain the conditions under which the Protestants would agree to reestablish peace in Germany. The King of the Romans, who had remained neutral in anticipation of the impending Turkish offensive in Hungary, promptly summoned Maurice of Saxony to a conference.[8] At Linz, on April 18, he learned that the price of peace would be in effect official recognition of Lutheranism in the Empire. As the consent of Charles and the Catholics was needed for any agreement, Ferdinand recommended that the Protestant terms be submitted to a meeting of all the Ger-

---

[8] Ferdinand's policies during the rebellion are carefully studied by G. Fischer, *Die persönliche Stellung und politische Lage König Ferdinands I vor und während der Passauer Verhandlungen des Jahres 1552* (Königsberg, 1891), 11 ff. On his relations with Maurice of Saxony consult F. A. von Langenn, *Moritz, Herzog und Churfürst zu Sachsen* (Leipzig, 1841), II, 338 ff.

man princes, Charles, and himself in May. He believed that an equitable solution "abolishing the dissensions and abuses of the German nation" might be reached at that time. Maurice accepted Ferdinand's proposition and promised Protestant attendance at a meeting to open on May 26 at Passau.

In the meantime, to strengthen their strategic and bargaining positions, the Protestant rebels continued their offensive against the Emperor. By the middle of May the conspirators had reached Innsbruck, forcing Charles to flee ignominiously across the border on the night of the nineteenth. One week later Protestant and Catholic princes assembled at Passau.[9] Ferdinand alone represented the Hapsburgs.

The terms submitted to the assembly by the Protestants were more moderate than expected by either Ferdinand or the Catholics. Maurice of Saxony demanded official recognition of Lutheranism pending the possible reconciliation of Catholic and Lutheran dogma by a council of the German nation. Should no mutually satisfactory compromise be reached, the Interim would be terminated and a formal peace treaty concluded between Lutherans and Catholics on the basis of religious and political equality.

The Protestant terms were designed to secure agreement at Passau rapidly and face Charles with a *fait accompli* he could not but accept. The leaders of the rebellion were cognizant of the desire of Ferdinand and the Catholics for peace. The King of the Romans had to contend with the Ottoman offensive in Hungary that started in March. The Turkish forces had reached Weisprim by April and Buda by the end of May. The expedition itself was insignificant in terms of the once formidable Ottoman marches on Hungary, yet it was nevertheless powerful enough to jeopardize successful implementation of the arrangements made at Weissenburg. Maurice was able to assess Ferdinand's position in April when he offered

[9] The negotiations preliminary to the conclusion of the Treaty of Passau are summarized and interpreted by G. Bonwetsch, *Geschichte des Passauischen Vertrages von 1552* (Göttingen, 1907), 49 ff.; Fischer, *Die persönliche,* 23 ff., W. Kühns, *Geschichte des Passauischen Vertrages 1552* (Göttingen, 1906), 38 ff.

Protestant cooperation against the Turks if Charles would accept the rebels' terms. As the King of the Romans appeared responsive, he repeated the offer at Passau. The Protestants also sought to appeal to Catholic prejudices and apparent eagerness to stabilize the German situation. They were aware that the Catholics opposed the Interim both as a theological compromise and an imperial weapon against the papacy. They interpreted Catholic abstinence from the recent conflict as a sign of disappointment with imperial policies and in the efficacy of military action as a means of resolving Germany's problems. The Protestants thought the idea of a national council restoring peace in Germany would appeal to the Catholics under the circumstances prevailing in May 1552.

The Protestants had accurately appraised the reaction of Ferdinand and the Catholics to their proposals. From as early as April the King of the Romans had decided for himself that a compromise peace should be concluded in Germany. Regardless of Lutheran promises of assistance and the advantages that pacification would entail for the realization of his plans in Hungary and regarding succession to the Empire, Ferdinand now excluded the possibility that any council could achieve a religious reconciliation. Continuing political instability was a most undesirable alternative in terms of Hapsburg policies in Europe; therefore, he endorsed the Protestant terms at Passau.[10] The Catholics agreed that the restoration of political peace and Catholic dogma unchanged by the Interim was worth the price asked by the Protestants. Charles, however, refused to accept the *fait accompli.*

The Emperor opposed any compromise that would recognize permanent religious division in Germany.[11] Regardless of the failure of the Interim and the Council of Trent to resolve outstanding theological differences, he had not despaired of an eventual conciliar solution. Thus, when faced with the Protestant terms and the de-

---

[10] See Ferdinand's correspondence during this period in Lanz, *Correspondenz*, III, 291 ff.; also Fischer's clear analysis of Ferdinand's position, Fischer, *Die persönliche*, 43 ff.

[11] Charles' position is most clearly outlined in his letter to Mary of Hungary of July 16, 1552, von Druffel, *Beiträge*, II, 681–686. See also his correspondence with Ferdinand in Lanz, *Correspondenz*, III, 318–327.

mands of Ferdinand and the Catholics for their acceptance, Charles refused to ratify them. However, considering his defeat in Germany, the war with Henry II, Ottoman activity in Hungary, and the united German position favoring religious compromise and restoration of peace, the Emperor presented a compromise solution of his own. He would consent to the free exercise of the Lutheran religion in Germany until a national council (over which he would preside) should reconsider the Interim and seek an equitable solution to Germany's political problems. He would not commit himself on future action in the case of the council's failing to solve the questions, except to emphasize his conciliatory intentions and determination to restore peace within the Empire.

Charles' reply disappointed the Protestant confederates and Ferdinand. The Protestants decided to force the Emperor to consent to their demands by resuming military action to be coordinated with that of the French troops fighting at Metz and Toulouse. Ferdinand, who had hoped to divert the Lutheran forces against the Turks in Hungary as soon as peace was reestablished in Germany, bombarded Charles with requests to accept the inevitable and approve the Protestant terms immediately. But the Emperor remained adamant. By mid-July he had rebuilt his military strength sufficiently to plan an offensive against Henry. He could therefore warn the Protestants to cease hostilities lest he divert his forces against them. He adopted an equally intransigent attitude toward Ferdinand's requests. Turkish activity in Hungary, the Emperor wrote his brother, did not justify concessions of the magnitude he had suggested. Nevertheless, as he did not wish to prolong the war in Germany and jeopardize Ferdinand's chances of securing assistance against the Turks in Hungary, he would renew his offer for a religious and political truce. Accordingly, he repeated his terms to the Protestants late in July. All but Albert Alcibiades accepted the Emperor's proposition as the basis of the Treaty of Passau on August 2.

Their choice was indeed limited.[12] The Protestants knew that continuing opposition to Charles' authority would be fatal to their

[12] A summary of the Protestants' reasons for acceptance may be found in the letter of Maurice of Saxony to his counselors, August 1, 1552, von Druffel, *Beiträge,* II, 713.

cause. In addition to certain military defeat they also risked aliena-
tion of the tacit support they had received from the German people
and Ferdinand. Defiance of the *Landfriede* and imperial authority
was unjustifiable even if temporarily condoned in times of grave
emergency. Charles' conciliatory offer, however, ended any "emergency" that might have existed in 1552. The foreseeable termination
of the Interim and the probability of a peaceful, if not definitive,
solution of Germany's problems satisfied the majority of the Lutherans and Catholics in the Empire. The Catholics in particular
endorsed the imperial position as they preferred postponement of a
formal religious peace with the Lutherans under the circumstances.
But even the Lutherans urged acceptance of Charles' terms and
immediate cessation of hostilities. A war against the Emperor in
alliance with a friend of the Infidel at a time when the Turks were
challenging the King of the Romans in Hungary was unpardon-
able. These pressures alone would probably have sufficed to make
the Protestants accept Charles' offer. Ferdinand's insistence made
agreement mandatory.

In August 1552 the Protestant leaders possessed a clear understanding of the forces that would eventually obtain permanent
recognition for Lutheranism in Germany.[13] As the principle of
compromise in religious and political affairs had been formally
accepted by Ferdinand, the Catholics, and even Charles, the Protestants rightly thought that the Treaty of Passau would become
the basis of an ultimate agreement. The Catholics had indicated
at Passau that they favored a compromise peace should the national
council fail to fulfill Charles' hopes for reconciliation, but they were
skeptical of success. Ferdinand was even more explicit in his endorsement of permanent recognition of Lutheranism as the basis
for reestablishment of peace in Germany. In urging acceptance of
Charles' offer, the King of the Romans assured the Protestants of
his determination to end religious and political strife. He would
persuade the Emperor to convene the council as soon as feasible,

---

[13] An excellent analysis of the factors leading to the Religious Peace of
Augsburg is by K. Brandi, "Passauer Vertrag und Augsburger Religionsfriede," *Historische Zeitschrift,* XCV (1905), 206 ff.

perhaps even convince him to renounce the conciliar plan altogether should the German and international situations make delay unwise. As King of the Romans he favored reestablishment of order in war-torn Germany; as King of Hungary he needed peace and support for the consolidation of his position, now challenged anew by the Turks.

The Protestant leaders found Ferdinand's arguments persuasive. It was doubtful that the Emperor could resist the general German clamor for peace or the entreaties of his brother even if he were able to summon a council in the near future. But the convocation of a council appeared unlikely in the summer of 1552 when both Henry and the Turks were readying themselves for prolonged warfare. Even if one were called, the other factors tending to help the Protestant cause should overcome Charles' opposition to granting recognition. Therefore, awaiting further developments, the Protestants accepted the Emperor's terms, ceased hostilities against him, and granted assistance to Ferdinand for defending his interests in Hungary. In August 1552 the Hapsburgs, Catholics, and Lutherans had apparently substituted compromise through peaceful negotiations for war as the most hopeful method of settling Germany's problems.

Subsequent events proved the wisdom of Protestant acceptance of the Treaty of Passau, for the forces working for religious and political pacification on Lutheran terms gained in strength after 1553. A combination of developments expedited the convening of the Diet of Augsburg at which the Lutherans secured permanent legal recognition in Germany. Foremost among them was Charles' abandonment of the conciliar plan under pressure from the King of the Romans. Beginning in 1553 Ferdinand could report only news that would force the Emperor to consent to a vitally needed permanent stabilization of the chaotic German situation.[14] His campaign to overcome Charles' resistance to a German pacification based on Protestant terms opened wth the forwarding of alarming reports on the activities of Albert of Brandenburg. The Protestant

[14] Consult Ferdinand's correspondence with Charles, Lanz, *Correspondenz*, III, 523 ff.

leader alone had rejected the Treaty of Passau and continued the war against the Emperor. After January 1553 all who opposed him, Catholic and Lutheran alike, became the targets of his military activities, which soon descended to the level of indiscriminate country-wide ravagings and plunderings by a growing rabble of rebellious German peasants. Fear of another peasant war mounted throughout 1553, resulting in united action by German princes against Albert. His ultimate defeat in 1554 did not, however, end the unrest among the peasantry or repair the devastation caused by his forays. Immediate restoration of order was considered by the German leaders, both Lutheran and Catholic, as well as Ferdinand, an essential prerequisite for a stable religious and political peace.

Accompanying these dire reports were relistings of Ferdinand's requirements in Hungary. The King of the Romans emphasized the unique opportunities that existed in 1553 for the realization of his Hungarian policy. The Turks, he argued, were on the defensive after their campaign of 1552. The withdrawal of the forces commanded by Achmet Pasha after a routine expedition was indicative of Ottoman weakness. Even more auspicious was Suleiman's refusal to nullify by force the Treaty of Weissenburg, as the repentant Isabella had requested in 1553. The Sultan would risk no war in Hungary for the restoration of the Zápolya dynasty at a time when another expedition against the Persian Shah appeared unavoidable; however, he also refused to recognize Ferdinand's claims to Hungary. A special ambassador sent to Constantinople in 1553 was bluntly informed that the Porte would maintain the *status quo* pending his further appraisal of the rival claims. But Ferdinand would not be balked. The time had come, he wrote Charles, early in 1554, to implement his demands for recognition through military action. He would launch an offensive against the Territory of Ofen during the anticipated Ottoman spring campaign in the Middle East and consolidate his gains to meet possible retaliatory action by the Porte. He seemed confident of success provided that adequate subsidies could be obtained. He was optimistic of German support as soon as a stable peace was concluded in the Empire. As Emperor and head of the House of Hapsburg, Charles should summon a Reichstag immediately to settle Germany's problems first, and second, to appropriate long-range subsidies for the achievement of Hapsburg policies in Hungary.

Charles resisted Ferdinand's entreaties until June 8, 1554.[15] While less and less convinced of the feasibility of theological compromise through conciliar action after the Treaty of Passau, the Emperor still hoped that a *modus operandi* might eventually be found. But the deterioration of the German situation in 1553 and early 1554 and his inability to bring to a close the war with Henry II all combined to erode his resistance to the permanent legal recognition of Lutheranism in the Empire. Therefore, early in June, he authorized Ferdinand to summon a Reichstag to seek the conclusion of a stable religious and political peace in Germany.[16] Neither the French war nor the state of his health (he wrote his brother) would permit his coming to Germany himself. Moreover, his conscience would never allow him personally to extent unconditional recognition to the heretical faith. Ferdinand must attempt a settlement of Germany's problems—he would not need the consent of the Emperor for any of his decisions since he could act in the all-powerful capacity of King of the Romans.

The imperial decision of June 8, 1554 resulted in Ferdinand's summoning a Diet forthwith. It assembled at Augsburg in November 1554.[17] The negotiations for a final settlement of the religious and political questions did not involve theological compromise. Catholics and Lutherans agreed on the futility of even attempting it. However, on September 25, 1555 the Religious Peace of Augsburg formally recorded the decision of the Reichstag by which Lutheranism was recognized as an official religion in Germany and legal equality granted to all worshippers of that faith. Appropriately enough, the Recess also registered the granting of subsidies against the Turks by the assembled estates.[18] The Protestants and the King of the Romans had both attained their goals.

[15] Consult Charles' correspondence with Ferdinand, Lanz, *Correspondenz,* III, 559 ff.

[16] See Charles' mandate in Lanz, *Correspondenz,* III, 622 ff.

[17] The best summary of the negotiations at Augsburg is by G. Wolf, *Der Augsburger Religionsfriede* (Stuttgart, 1890), 1 ff.

[18] Schmauss, *Neue Sammlung,* II[1], 14 ff.

Although the Religious Peace of Augsburg was not immediately related to Turkish military activity against the Hapsburgs, the Ottoman challenge to Ferdinand's interests in Hungary considerably influenced the final outcome of the Protestant struggle for recognition in Germany. In 1548, after their defeat in the Schmalkaldian War and forced acceptance of the Interim terms, the Protestants felt their cause in serious jeopardy. In 1552 the leaders of a victorious Protestant conspiracy against Charles obtained *de facto* recognition for their religion by the Treaty of Passau. This dramatic change in the fortunes of the German Lutherans may be ascribed to several factors which all contributed to the conclusion of the Religious Peace of Augsburg.

The period 1547–1552 recorded the failure of Charles' German policy. His futile insistence on radical Church reform resulted in the Interim. By 1552 the enforcement of this unsuitable compromise had alienated the Catholics. His insistence on Philip's succession as King of the Romans in 1551 alienated Ferdinand. In 1552 the King of the Romans had resumed activity in Hungary which had been suspended since 1543. The defeated Protestants exploited the contradictions of the imperial policy. In 1552 when the carefully planned rebellion took place, the Protestants benefited first from the neutrality and later the support of the Catholics and Ferdinand. Indeed, the realization of Ferdinand's secular aims in the Empire and Hungary made him become an advocate of the Protestants' cause at Passau and in subsequent years. With Catholic endorsement, he persuaded Charles to admit defeat. Unable to withstand the pressure for peace in Germany and unwilling to frustrate the realization of Ferdinand's plans in Hungary, the Emperor had to acknowledge in June 1554 that the concessions which the Protestants had been able to secure since 1532 could not be eradicated by wars or councils as long as unity of purpose and action did not obtain in Christian Europe or in the Holy Roman Empire.

Chapter VI

Conclusion

On September 25, 1555 the Lutherans obtained official recognition for their religious and political organization in Germany. This triumph could be attributed to the ingenuity, astuteness, and perseverance of their leaders, past and present. Some of the delegates to the Diet of Augsburg must also have realized their debt to Maximilian I, for through his bequest to his successors the establishment of Lutheranism in Germany had been greatly facilitated. Indeed, the entire course of the Reformation might have been different had Charles and Ferdinand yielded priority to German affairs over the consolidating of their family inheritance.

Charles became Holy Roman Emperor in 1519. Like his grandfather before him, he failed to understand the full significance of the Lutheran revolt. Instead of giving his undivided attention to German problems, the Emperor departed for Italy, leaving a council of regency under the eighteen-year-old Ferdinand to enforce the harsh Edict of Worms. The decision to leave Ferdinand as Staathalter was unfortunate. The younger Hapsburg had little understanding of the German situation; moreover, he was primarily interested in defending Hungary from Turkish invasion. With Charles in Italy and Ferdinand preoccupied with the fate of the eastern Hapsburg possessions, a group of princes and cities, discerning the opportunities offered by Lutheranism as a vehicle for the realization of their secular ambitions, proclaimed themselves adherents of the new faith and prepared to exploit the unsettled conditions in Germany. In 1526, the early followers of Luther scored their first major success. As a result of Ferdinand's need for assistance against the

Turks and the Catholic insistence on solving the religious question by a Christian council, they obtained official guarantees for the security of their religion. The year 1526 was one of decisive importance for German Protestantism, since it was then that the Emperor endorsed the principle of conciliar solution of the Lutheran question. Through this decision Charles again relegated German affairs to a position subsidiary to the fulfillment of Hapsburg secular policies in Europe and thereby furthered the Lutheran plans for consolidation and expansion. Attempted settlement of Germany's problems would be greatly delayed because of papal opposition to the summoning of a council and Hapsburg involvement in Italy and Hungary. Thus, while Charles was trying to gain control over Italy and persuade the Pope to convoke a council, and Ferdinand was pursuing an aggressive policy in Hungary, Lutheranism was making headway in Germany. By 1529, the movement had gained enough strength to oblige the Emperor to abandon the war in Italy and try to subdue the heresy. In 1530, Charles, with the support of Ferdinand and the Catholics, pronounced a death sentence on Protestantism at the Diet of Augsburg. With peace reestablished in Western Europe a solution to the religious question appeared possible. But the Protestants won a reprieve, primarily because of a powerful Ottoman offensive against Hungary and the Empire. Charles and Ferdinand could interdict Lutheranism at Speyer and Augsburg but could not dispense with its assistance when their secular interests in Eastern Europe and the very security of the Empire itself appeared in grave danger. In return for support against the Turks the Emperor was prepared to guarantee the existence of Lutheranism until the meeting of a council. The imperial decision of 1532 represented a decisive victory for the Lutherans, for, despite the temporary nature of the Religious Peace of Nürnberg, neither Charles nor Ferdinand was able to revoke it for nearly fifteen years.

In 1532, following the withdrawal of the Turks from Güns, Charles returned to Western Europe to spend the next decade guarding his possessions against the French king and the Turkish fleet. The struggle against Lutheranism was delegated to Ferdinand and the papacy. As King of the Romans, the younger Hapsburg was to arrest the spread of the heresy by temporal means; as head of the Christian Church, the Pope was to summon a free council that would remove the obstacles to the Lutherans' rejoining the Catholic fold. But the Emperor's plans were miscalculated. The papacy, fearing diminution of its temporal and spiritual power through reform of the Church, refused to convene the council; Ferdinand, unwilling to forfeit his claims to Hungary, did not succeed in arresting the growth of Protestantism. The Lutherans profited by the failure of the papacy and Ferdinand to fulfill their obligations—by 1539 they were powerful enough to secure far-reaching guarantees for their religious and political existence in Germany. But, as in the past, Lutheran advances stimulated intensified efforts to counteract and nullify them.

In 1541, Charles sought spiritual and political reunification of a divided Germany. The attempt failed because the religious creeds and political aspirations of Catholics and Protestants were irreconcilable. Consolidation and expansion of Lutheranism had to be tolerated by the Emperor because of the exigencies of the international situation. The activities of the Turks in Hungary and the Mediterranean and their ally Francis I in Italy forced Charles to renew and extend the guarantees which the Lutherans had extracted from Ferdinand in 1539 under similar circumstances. Only in 1546 were the Hapsburgs freed to concentrate on German affairs, to try to recover the ground they had lost to the Lutherans during the preceding twenty years. With Western and Eastern Europe both at peace, Charles and Ferdinand were enabled to attempt German reunification by force and conciliar action.

Victorious in the Schmalkaldian War, the Hapsburgs could dictate their terms to the defeated enemy. Until the summoning of a free council the Augsburg Interim and Charles' presence in Germany were intended to assure the reestablishment of religious and political unity until the summoning of a free council. But reunification was no longer possible. The theologically defective Interim and the unyielding stand of the papacy rendered spiritual reconciliation out of the question. Secular considerations affecting Hapsburg interests in Germany, Western Europe and Hungary forced imperial acceptance of Germany's permanent religious and political division among Lutherans and Catholics in 1555. This division could probably have been avoided had Charles and Ferdinand assigned German affairs priority over the realization of secular ambitions outside the Empire. In this respect Charles was the lesser offender.

The Emperor was at all times determined to prevent a permanent establishment of Lutheranism in Germany. But he was possessed by an unrealistic imperial idea that political reunification of Europe under his own leadership was a prerequisite for the restoration of spiritual unity in Western Christendom. Giving preference to the realization of the secular goals of the Hapsburgs was thus justified in terms of his ultimate aim, the reestablishment of the universal church within the Holy Roman Empire. Only in 1554, when the Council of Trent had rejected his conciliar views and the German Catholics and Ferdinand himself had joined the ranks of the traditional opponents of his secular policies, did he acknowledge the failure of the imperial idea and the seriousness of the consequences of that failure for Germany. Then only did he fully realize the significance of his compromises with the Lutherans. Indeed, his absence from Germany during the formative years of the Reformation gave the Lutherans an opportunity to defy imperial authority and gain adherents for their faith in spite of the Edict of Worms. His decision of 1532 to compromise with the Protestants rather than increase German disunity when the Turks were threatening Hungary and the Empire resulted in the Religious Peace of Nürnberg. His *de jure* confirmation of the Compact of Cadan and *de facto* acceptance of the Frankfurt Anstand weakened the attempts of the Catholics to enforce the provisions of the Recess of Augsburg and Religious Peace of Nürnberg and allowed the Protestants to continue expansion in the Empire. Finally, his decision of 1541 to accord precedence to the protection of Hapsburg secular interests in Hungary and the West over the urgent problem of arresting the growth of Lutheranism gave the Protestants another five years to strengthen their position in Germany.

Although Charles' unintentional contribution to the progress of the Reformation was considerable, it was nevertheless not as great as that of Ferdinand. Ferdinand was not motivated by the idealistic imperial idea, but by practical political considerations. His main concern was to protect his Hungarian inheritance from Ottoman conquest and usurpation by John Zápolya and his successors. Germany's problems were of lesser importance to him, as he considered them to be Charles' ultimate responsibility and in addition, shared the Emperor's view that they could be eventually solved by a council. Under the circumstances he did not hesitate to advocate (and occasionally himself take) measures that would temporarily benefit the Protestant cause if they also advanced his secular interests in Hungary.

In 1526, when Hapsburg claims to Hungary appeared gravely jeopardized by the joint actions of Suleiman and Zápolya, Ferdinand approved the Recess of Speyer. To secure peace in Germany and Lutheran support for his plans in Hungary in the thirties, he recognized the conquest of Würtemberg at Cadan and ratified the progress of the Reformation at Frankfurt. In 1542 he decided that reconquest of the Territory of Ofen justified extension of the concessions granted the Lutherans by Charles at Regensburg. Ferdinand recognized the failure of Hapsburg policies in Germany by 1552. But, unlike the Emperor, he was willing to acknowledge the realities of the German situation at that time. He would not allow artificial solutions to interfere with the realization of his secular aims. Therefore he remained neutral during the rebellion of 1552, favored pacification on Protestant terms at Passau, and induced Charles' reluctant acceptance of the principles of Augsburg in 1554.

The significance of the concessions made to the Lutherans by the Hapsburgs because of considerations of secular policy not directly connected with German affairs assumes major proportions when related to other factors responsible for the success of the Reformation in Germany. Whether or not the Lutheran movement could have been suppressed or arrested by strict enforcement of the various measures designed for this purpose is doubtful. The princes' and cities' tradition of resistance to imperial authority, the religious and economic appeal of Lutheranism, German opposition to Roman policies, and, perhaps most significantly, the pope's reluctance to summon a free council all created conditions favorable for the survival of Lutheranism. It is evident, however, that the Hapsburgs' neglect of German affairs and readiness to compromise when beset by international pressures and exigencies was the single most important factor in expediting the process of consolidation, expansion and formal recognition of Lutheranism in 1555. It is also evident that from an early date Lutheran leaders appreciated the significance of the international commitments of the Hapsburgs and the vast benefits that might be derived from their exploitation. It is in this connection that the Ottoman Turks assumed a major role in the history of the German Reformation.

The Turks, together with the French, were the principal opponents of Hapsburg hegemony in Europe in the first half of the sixteenth century. As an Eastern power expanding westward, the Ottoman Turks came into conflict with a Western power expanding eastward. The unavoidable clash occurred over Hungary, the coveted state separating the Hapsburg and Ottoman empires. The struggle for Hungary had continued virtually without intermission since 1526. Its most dramatic manifestations were the sieges of Vienna in 1529 and Güns in 1532. It also took the form of lesser Turkish military action in 1541, 1543, and 1552 and in skirmishes at frequent intervals. More significant than military activity per se was its ultimate cause: Ottoman rejection of Hapsburg claims to Hungary. As long as this situation existed, as long as the Porte supported such rival claimants as John Zápolya and John Sigismund or assumed direct control over central Hungary as it did in 1541, the conflict between Hapsburg and Turk would continue. While centering on Hungary, the conflict between the two powers expanded as the century progressed. As a naval power in the Mediterranean in the early thirties, the Turks challenged Hapsburg supremacy in North Africa and west of the Adriatic; as allies of Francis I after 1535 they fomented political instability in Western Europe and made the realization of Charles' imperial plans more and more illusory.

The Protestants readily linked the problems presented to the Hapsburgs by direct and indirect Ottoman aggression with their struggle for survival, consolidation, and expansion in Germany. Most significantly, they utilized the Hapsburg dependence on German assistance for the protection of the Empire and the attainment of Hungarian aims to further their own cause. Almost all major concessions wrested from the Hapsburgs since 1526 were connected with Ottoman activities in Eastern and Western Europe, and the all-important Lutheran campaign for legal recognition in Germany exploited the insoluble Hapsburg-Ottoman conflict over Hungary. The Recess of Speyer of 1526, the Religious Peace of Nürnberg, the Compact of Cadan, the Frankfurt Anstand, the Declaration of Regensburg, the Recess of Speyer of 1542, the Treaty of Passau, and the Religious Peace of Augsburg—all milestones in the Protestant struggle for recognition and the course of the German Reformation —were deeply influenced by the ebb and flow of Ottoman aggression.

It is paradoxical that the success of the Reformation in Germany should be so closely linked with the fortunes of the generally feared and despised Turk. But the Protestant leaders, despite limitations imposed upon them by theological restrictions and German abhorrence of the Infidel, relentlessly exploited the opportunities arising from the secular conflict between Hapsburg and Ottoman. Their perseverance in pursuing such a policy accurately reflects the nature and importance of the Turkish impact on the German Reformation. The Turks diverted the attention of the Hapsburgs from German affairs and made them dependent on Protestant cooperation for the realization of their secular ambitions in Europe, particularly Hungary. The consolidation, expansion, and legitimizing of Lutheranism in Germany by 1555 should be attributed to Ottoman imperialism more than to any other single factor.

Bibliography

Index

Bibliography

(The bibliography is limited to works specifically used in preparing this study.)

I. BIBLIOGRAPHICAL AIDS

Brandi, K., *Kaiser Karl V.* 2 v. München, 1937–1941. (Volume II, *Quellen und Erörterungen*, contains all the bibliographical references pertinent to the author's biography of Charles V. It is especially valuable for references to archival materials and for excerpts therefrom.)

Hohenemser, P., *Flugschriftensammlung Gustav Freitag.* Frankfurt am Main, 1925. (The most complete bibliography of German *Flugschriften*.)

Kabdebo, H., *Bibliographie zur Geschichte der beiden Türkenbelagerungen Wiens, 1529 und 1683.* Wien, 1876. (Contains references to contemporary accounts and later histories of the siege of 1529.)

Michoff, N. V., *Sources bibliographiques sur l'histoire de la Turquie et de la Bulgarie.* 4 v. Sofia, 1914–1934. (The only semiadequate bibliography of the history of the Ottoman Empire. Limited to secondary materials.)

Schottenloher, K., *Bibliographie zur deutschen Geschichte im Zeitalter der Glaubenspaltung, 1517–1585.* 6 v. Leipzig, 1933–1940. (An exhaustive bibliography of printed materials relevant to the history of Germany from the times of Maximilian I to 1585.)

Wolf, G., *Quellenkunde der deutschen Reformationsgeschichte.* 2 v. Gotha, 1915–1922.

II. PRIMARY SOURCES

A. Public Documents, Political Correspondence, Collections of Sources

Aktenstücke und Briefe zur Geschichte Kaiser Karl V. K. Lanz, ed. Wien, 1853. (A miscellaneous collection covering the first years of Charles' reign.)

"Aktenstücke zur Politik Kaiser Karl V im Herbst 1541," W. Friedensburg, ed., *Archiv für Reformationsgeschichte,* 29 (1932), 35–66.

"Aktenstücke zu den Religionsverhandlungen des Reichstages zu Regensburg 1532," J. Ficker, ed., *Zeitschrift für Kirchengeschichte,* XII (1890–91), 583–618.

Beiträge zur Politischen, Kirchlichen und Cultur-Geschichte der sechsletzten Jahrhunderte. J. J. I. von Döllinger, ed. 3 v. Regensburg, 1862–63. (Volume I, *Dokumente zur Geschichte Karls V, Philipps II und ihrer Zeit,* contains a collection of miscellaneous documents pertinent to the reign of Charles.)

Beiträge zur Reichsgeschichte, 1546–1555. A. von Druffel, ed. 4 v. München, 1873–1896. (Contains a large number of *Briefe* and *Akten* from 1546 to 1555.)

Briefe an Kaiser Karl V, geschrieben von seinem Beichtvater in den Jahren 1530–32. G. Heine, ed. Berlin, 1848. (The letters of García de Loaysa to Charles.)

Briefe und Akten zu der Geschichte des Religionsgespräches zu Marburg 1529 und des Reichstages zu Augsburg 1530. F. W. Schirmacher, ed. Gotha, 1876.

von Bucholtz, F. B., *Geschichte der Regierung Ferdinand des Ersten.* 9 v. Wien, 1831–39. (Volume IX, *Urkunden-Band,* contains a vast selection of documents pertaining to the history of Ferdinand.)

Correspondance de Charles-Quint et d'Adrien VI. L. P. Gachard, ed. Brussels, 1859.

Correspondance de l'Empereur Maximilien Ier et de Marguerite d'Autriche, sa fille, gouvernante des Pays-Bas, de 1507 à 1519. A. J. G. le Glay, ed. 2 v. Paris, 1839.

Correspondence of the Emperor Charles V and his Ambassadors at the Courts of England and France. W. Bradford, ed. London, 1850.

Correspondenz des Kaisers Karl V. K. Lanz, ed. 3 v. Leipzig, 1844–46.

Des Heiligen Römischen Reichs Teutscher Nation Reichstagsstaat von Anno 1500 bis 1509 unter Kaysers Maximiliani I Regierung. J. J. Müller, ed. Jena, 1709. (Contains valuable miscellaneous materials on the history of the Diets of the first decade of the sixteenth century.)

Des Heil Römischen Reichs Teutscher Nation Reichs Tags Theatrum wie selbigis unter Keyser Maximilian I. J. J. Müller, ed. 2 v. Jena, 1718–19. (Selections from the negotiations of the Diets in the times of Maximilian I.)

Deutsche Reichstagsakten unter Kaiser Karl V. A. Kluckhohn et al., ed. 5 v. Gotha, 1893–1935. (The last volume is published in two parts. This covers only the period 1517–1529. The documents for the Diet of Speyer of 1526 have not been published.)

"Die Depeschen des Venezianischen Gesandten Nicolo Tiepolo über die Religionsfrage auf dem Augsburger Reichstage 1530," J. von Walter, ed., *Abhandlungen der Gesellschaft der Wissenschaften zu Göttingen* (Philologisch-Historische Klasse) Neue Folge, XXIII (1928), 1–86.

Die Korrespondenz Ferdinands I. W. Bauer and R. Lacroix, ed. 2 v. Wien, 1912–1938. (Ends with the year 1530. Volume II is published in two parts.)

Von Druffel, A., *Kaiser Karl V und die Römische Curie 1544–1546.* 4 v. München, 1877–1890. (The appendixes to volume I, pp. 106–132; volume II, pp. 38–85; volume III, pp. 62–111; and volume IV, pp. 47–97, contain documents pertinent to the conciliar policies of Charles and the papacy.)

Epistolae Imperatorum et Regnum Hungariae Ferdinandi Primi et Maximiliani Secundi ad suos in Porta Ottomanica Oratores. I. F. de Miller, ed. Pest, 1808. (Begins with the year 1553.)

Epistolarum Turcicarum Variorum et Diversorum Authorum. N. Reusner, ed. 4 v. Franckfurt am Main, 1598–1600.

"Extraits de la correspondance diplomatique de Jean-Thomas de Langosco, Comte de Stroppiana, et de Claude Malopera, ambassadeurs du Duc de Savoie à la cour de Charles-Quint. 1546–1559," G. Greppi, ed., *Compte Rendu des Séances de la Commission Royale d'Histoire,* 2e série, XII (Bruxelles, 1859), 117–271.

Förstemann, K. E., *Urkundenbuch zu der Geschichte des Reichstages zu Augsburg im Jahre 1530.* 2 v. Halle, 1833–35. (The appendix to volume I, pp. 201–533 and the entire volume II contain materials important for the study of the Augsburg Confession.)

Frankfurts Reichscorrespondenz nebst andern verwandten Aktenstücken von 1376–1519. J. Janssen, ed. 2 v. Freiburg im Breisgau, 1863–1872. (Volume II is published in two parts, the second of which covers the period 1486–1519.)

Friedensburg, W., *Der Reichstag zu Speier 1526 im Zusammenhang der politischen und kirchlichen Entwicklung Deutschlands im Reformationszeitalter,* Berlin, 1887. (Appendix II, pp. 497–581, contains a selection of miscellaneous archival materials.)

"Kardinal Lorenzo Campeggio auf dem Reichstage zu Augsburg 1530," S. Ehses, ed., *Römische Quartalschrift für Christliche Altertumskunde und für Kirchengeschichte,* XVII (1903), XX (1906), XXI (1907), 383–406, 54–80, 114–139. (A collection of dispatches from April to December 1530.)

Von Langenn, F. A., *Moritz, Herzog und Churfürst zu Sachsen.* 2 v. Leipzig, 1841. (Appendix to volume II, pp. 175–367, contains miscellaneous materials connected with the history of Maurice of Saxony.)

Maurenbrecher, W., *Karl V und die deutschen Protestanten 1545–1555.* Düsseldorf, 1865. (The appendix: 3*–184*, contains materials from the Spanish archives of Simancas.)

Mayer, E. W., "Forschungen zur Politik Karls V während des Augsburger Reichstages von 1530," *Archiv für Reformationsgeschichte,* 13 (1916), 40–73, 124–146. (The appendixes: 61–73, 133–146 contain miscellaneous materials concerning Charles' policy in 1530.)

Mentz, G., *Johann Friedrich der Grossmütige,* 3 v. Jena, 1903–08. (The appendixes to volume I, pp. 95–142, and volume III, pp. 346–575, contain documents pertinent to the history of John Frederick of Saxony.)

Négociations de la France dans le Levant. E. Charrière, ed. 4 v. Paris, 1848–1860. (Volumes I and II contain materials covering the period 1522–1555.)

Négociations diplomatiques entre la France et l'Autriche durant les trentes premières années du XVIe siècle. A. J. G. le Glay, ed. 2 v. Paris, 1845.

Neue und vollständigere Sammlung der Reichsabschiede welche von den Zeiten Kayser Conrads des II bis Jetzo auf den Teutschen Reichs-Tägen abgefasset worden. J. J. Schmauss, ed. 2 v. Franckfurt am Mayn, 1747. (Both volumes I and II are published in two parts.)

Neues Urkundenbuch zur Geschichte der evangelischen Kirchen-Reformation. K. E. Förstemann, ed. Hamburg, 1842. (Contains miscellaneous materials covering the period 1520–1545.)

Nuntiaturberichte aus Deutschland 1533–1559. W. Friedensburg *et al.,* ed. 12 v. Gotha, 1892–1912. (These do not go beyond May 1552.)

Papiers d'Etat du Cardinal de Granvelle. C. Weiss, ed. 9 v. Paris, 1841–1852. (Volumes I–IV cover the period through 1555.)

Politische Correspondenz der Stadt Strassburg im Zeitalter der Reformation. H. Virck *et al.,* ed. 5 v. Strassburg, 1882–1928. (Volume IV is published in two parts.)

Politische Korrespondenz des Herzogs und Kurfürsten Moritz von Sachsen. E. Brandenburg, ed. 2 v. Leipzig, 1900–04. (Volume II is published in two parts.)

Quellensammlung zur Geschichte der deutschen Reichsverfassung im Mittelalter und Neuzeit. K. Zeumer, ed. Leipzig, 1904. (A miscellaneous collection.)

Recueil des lettres de l'Empereur Charles-Quint qui sont conservées dans les Archives du Palais de Monaco. H. L. Labande, ed. Monaco, 1910. (Letters written by Charles to the ruler of Monaco, Augustin Grimaldi, between 1524 and 1544.)

Recueil des Traitez. J. Bernard, ed. 2 v. Amsterdam, 1700. (Volume II contains diplomatic treaties of the period 1435–1600.)

Relationen venetianischer Botschafter über Deutschland und Österreich im sechszehnten Jahrhundert. J. Fiedler, ed. Wien, 1870.

Relations des Ambassadeurs Vénitiens sur Charles-Quint et Philippe II. L. P. Gachard, ed. Brussels, 1855.

Relazioni degli Ambasciatori Veneti al Senato. E. Alberi, ed. 15 v. Firenze, 1839–1863. (Volumes I–III of Series I contain reports on Charles and Ferdinand; volume I of Series III contains reports on the Ottoman Empire.)

Rassow, P., *Die Kaiser-Idee Karls V.* Berlin, 1932. (The appendixes, pp. 399–439, contain miscellaneous materials from the period 1530–38.)

Roth, F., "Zur Geschichte des Reichstages zu Regensburg im Jahre 1541," *Archiv für Reformationsgeschichte,* 2 (1904–05), 250–307; 3 (1905–06), 18–64. (Appendix of part I, pp. 270–307, and all of part II contain a selection from the official correspondence between Augsburg city officials and their representatives at the Diet of Regensburg.)

Staatspapiere zur Geschichte des Kaisers Karl V. K. Lanz, ed. Stuttgart, 1845. (A miscellaneous collection.)

Ueber die Türkenkriege, namentlich des sechszehnten Jahrhunderts. E. Münch, ed. Zürich, 1821. (A collection of miscellaneous materials related to the Turkish wars of the sixteenth century.)

Urkunden und Aktenstücke zur Geschichte der Verhältnisse zwischen Oesterreich, Ungern und der Pforte im XVI. und XVII. Jahrhunderts. A. von Gevay, ed. 3 v. Wien, 1838–1842. (Covers only the period from 1527 to 1541.)

Venetianische Depeschen vom Kaiserhofe. G. Turba, ed. 3 v. Wien, 1889–1895. (Covers the period from 1538 to 1555.)

Westermann, A., *Die Türkenhilfe und die politisch-kirchlichen Parteien auf dem Reichstag zu Regensburg 1532.* Heidelberg, 1910. (The appendix, pp. 172–237, contains selections from the negotiations at the Diet of Regensburg.)

B. Private Correspondence

"Briefe an Desiderius Erasmus von Rotterdam," J. Förstemann and O. Günther, eds., *Beihefte zum Zentralblatt für Bibliothekswesen,* XXVII, Leipzig, 1904. (Letters from German humanists to Erasmus, 1520–1535, bearing in part on Turkish affairs.)

Briefwechsel Landgraf Philipps des Grossmüthigen von Hessen mit Bucer. M. Lenz, ed. 3 v. Leipzig, 1880–1891. (Begins with the year 1529.)

Failde, J. V., *La Emperatriz Isabel.* Madrid, 1917. (Appendix I, pp. 325–402, contains "Correspondencia inédita de Carlos I y la emperatriz Isabel, desde el 10 de julio de 1529 hasta el 21 de septiembre de 1532.")

C. Contemporary Literature: Writings of Humanists, Flugschriften, Zeitungen, etc.

Ain Anschlag wie man dem Türcke widerstand thun mag. n.p., 1522.

Abschrifft eines brieffs von Constantinopel auss welichem man zuernemen hat welcher gestalt der Gross Türck seine Priester und Doctores hat lassen umbringen auss ursachen das sie bestendiger weyss bekant und mit ursachen bekrefftiget haben Das Christliche Gesetz und Glaube warhafftig Das Machometisch aber falsch sey. n.p., 1539.

Ain Ermanung wider die Türcken. n.p., 1522.

Ain gründtlicher und warhaffter bericht was sich under der belagerung Stat Wyen Newlich im MDXXIX Jar zwyschen denen inn Wyen und Torcken begeben und zugetragen hat. n.p., n.d.

Ain Sendbrief wie sych der turckisch kaysser so grausamlich für die stat Rodis belegert und gewonnen hat. Augsburg, 1523.

Anschlag wider die grawsamen und blutdürstigen Tyranney der Türcken. n.p., 1541.

Apologia cuiusdam Regiae Famae Studiosi. Lutetiae, 1551.

Apologia Darin Koenigklicher Maiestat zu Frankreich gut geruecht vertheydingt unnd berantwort wuert. n.p., 1552.

Aufzug aines Brieffs wie einer so in der Türckey wonhafft seinem Freund in dise Land geschriben. n.p., 1526 (?).

Bando dele processioni per la unione de principi Christiani contra Turchi. Rome, 1518.

Brant, S., *At divum Maximilianum Caesarem invictissimum cunctosque Christiani nomines principes et populos naenia in Thurcarum nyciteria cum arripiendae in eosdem expeditionis exhortatione.* Strassburg, 1518.

—— *Narrenschiff.* ed. F. Zarnke. Leipzig, 1854.

Brentius, J., *Homiliae Viginti due, sub incursionem Turcarum in Germaniam, ad populos dicte.* Wittemberg, 1532.

—— *Wie sich Prediger und Leyden halten sollen so der Turck das deutsche land uberfalle wuerde.* Wittemberg, 1531.

Charles V, *The Autobiography of Charles V.* London, 1862.

Cnusti, H., *Von geringen herkommen schentlichem leben schmehlichem ende des Türckischen Abgots Machomets.* n.p., 1542.

Cochlaeus, J., *Dialogus de bello contra Turcas, in antilogias Lutheri per Joannem Cochleum.* Leipzig, 1529.

Copey unnd lautter Abschrifft ains warhafftigen Sendtbrieffs wie der Türkisch Kayser Solyman disen sein yetz gegenwürtigen Anzug wider die Christenheit geordnet von Constantinopel aussgezogen und gen Kriechischen Weyssenburg ankomen ist. n.p., 1532.

Copia ains brieffs aus Adrianopoli der innhalt der bindnuss und freunndtschafft So der Sophi mit dem grossen Tartero widern Türcken Gemacht hat. MDXXXIX. n.p., 1539.

Coptius, F., *Ad Caesarem pro Christiana republica de concordia Principum adversus Turcas.* Rome, 1523.

Cronica abconterfayung und entwerffung der Türckey, von einem Sibenburger in latein beschriben, durch Sebastian Frank verteuscht. Nürennberg(?), 1530.

Cuspinianus, J., *Oratio Protreptica Ad sacri Rom. Imp. Principes ut bellum suscipiant contra Turcum, cum descriptione conflictus nuper in Hungaria facti quo periit Rex Hungariae Ludovicus.* Wien, 1527(?).

Des Türcken erschröckenliche belegerung der Stat und Schloss Günss und des selben nach zwelff verlorn Stürmen abzug. n.p., 1532.

Dick, L., *Oratio ad Carolum Romanorum Imperatorem Augustum contra Thurcas.* n.p., 1521.

Die Eroberung der Stat Affrica. n.p., 1550

Die historischen Volkslieder der Deutschen vom 13 bis 16 Jahrhundert. ed. R. von Liliencron. 5 v. Leipzig, 1865–69.

Bibliography 127

Dietrich, V., *Wie man das volk zur Buss und ernstlichen gebet wider die Türcken auff der Cantzel vermanen sol.* Nuremberg, 1542.

Drei Denkschriften über die orientalische Frage von Papst Leo X, König Franz I von Frankreich und Kaiser Maximilian I aus dem Jahre 1517. J. W. Zinkeisen, ed. Gotha, 1854.

Eck, J., *Sperandam esse in brevi victoriam adversum Turcam.* Augsburg, 1532.

Ein gemeyne Predig zu den Kriegszleuten so wider die unglaublichen kriegenwoellen. n.p., 1542.

Ein kurtze Christliche Ermannung wie man inn disen geferlichsten zeitten sich zu Gott keren und dem Türcken obsigen moege. n.p., 1542.

Ein Sermon vo dem Turckenzug. n.p., 1532.

Ein Summari der Türckischen Botschafft werbung an die Herrschaft zu Venedig. n.p., 1537.

Erasmus, D., *Utilissima consultatio de Bello Turcis inferendo.* Antverpiae, 1530.

Erinnerung der verschulten plagen. n.p., 1528.

Ernstliche Newe zeytung so sich zwischen Kaiserlich unnd Künigklichen Maiestaten dem Babst Herrschafft zu Venedig und anders tails dem Türcken zugetragen. n.p., 1537.

Faber, J., *Oratio de Origine, Potentia, ac Tyrannide Thurcorum.* n.p., 1528.

Fontanus, J., *Ad Adrianum Pontificem Epistola elegantissima.* Tübingen, 1523.

——— *De bello Rhodio libri tres.* Rome, 1524.

Gengenbach, P., *Pamphilius Gengenbach, SRF.* ed. K. Goedeke. Hanover, 1856.

Gesta Impiorum per Francos sive Gesta Francorum per Impios exvarijs Auctoribus maioribus codecta. Rhenopoli, 1532.

Gjorgjevic, B., *De afflictione tam captivorum quam etiam sub Turcae tributo viuentium Christianorum.* Antverpiae, 1544.

——— *De Turcarum moribus epitome.* Lugduni, 1555.

——— *De Turcarum ritu et caeremoniis.* Antwerpiae, 1544.

Gute zeyttung von der Christlichen Armata eroberung Castellonouo und Rixana. n.p., 1539.

Heimliche anschlag und fürnemung des türckischen kaysers wan er Rodis eroberte. Augsburg, 1523.

Hessus, E., *Divo ac invicto Imp. Caes. Carolo V. Augusto Germaniam ingredienti urbis Norimbergae gratulatoria acclamatio. Ad cundem de bello contra Turcas suscipiendo adhortatio.* Nürnberg, 1530.

"Historische Lieder des 16. und 18. Jahrhundert," J. von Zahn, ed., *Steiermärkische Geschichtsblätter,* V (1884), 245–255.

Historische Volkslieder aus dem sechszehnten Jahrhundert. P. M. Körner, ed. Stuttgart, 1840.

Jonas, J., *Das Siebende Capitel Danielis, von des Türcken Gottes lesterung und schrecklicher mörderey, mit unterricht Justi Jonae.* Wittemberg, 1530.

Kriegsruestuge und Heerzuegt des wüterichen Türckischen Keysers. n.p., 1532.

von Kronberg, H., *Eyn sendbrieff an Babst Adrianum.* Wittemberg, 1523.

Ladislaus of Macedonia, Bishop of Varad, *Oratio invictissimum Romanorum Imperatorem Carolum V.* n.p., n.d.

Literaturdenkmäler aus Ungarns Tükenzeit. F. Babinger, ed. Berlin, 1917.

Locher, J., *Libri:Panegyrici ad Maximilianum imperatorem, Tragedia de Turcis et suldano, Dialogus de heresiarchis.* Strassburg, 1497.

—— *Spectaculum a Jacobo Lochner more tragico effigiatum.* Ingolstadt(?), 1502(?).

Luther, M., *D. Martin Luthers Büchlein vom Kriege wider den Türken und Heerpredigt wider den Türken im Jahre 1529.* ed. D. Kahnis. Leipzig, 1854.

—— *D. Martin Luthers Werke.* Weimar, 1883—.

—— *Works of Martin Luther.* 6 v. Philadelphia, 1915–1932.

Naw getzeiten von dem Turcken durch den konig von Neapolis keiserlicher maiestat zugeschickt. Augsburg, 1518.

Newe Zeitung. Was sich in Africa im MDXLIII Jar mit Einnemung und Eroberung des Koenigreychs Tremetzen verlaufen hat. n.p., 1543.

Newe zeyttung und warhafte anzaygung wie die streif send rott des Türkischen Tyrannen und verfolger des Christlichen pluets auss hilff und gnad des algemeinen Gots durch die unsern erlegt und umgebracht am 18 Septembris geschehen. n.p., 1532.

Newe zeitung von der Tuerkischen kriegsruestung so jtzige Winter um Ungern gebracht. n.p., 1551.

Newe zeytung von veraynigung und frid zwischen Rö.Kö. Maiestat und dem grossmaechtigesten Türckischen Kayser in kurtz verschiner zeyt bescheben. n.p., 1533.

Pimpinelli, V., *Oratio Augustae habita XI. Kal. Iulij 1530.* Augsburg, 1530.

Rerum Germanicarum Scriptores. M. Freher and B. Struve, eds. 3 v. Argentorati, 1717.

Sendschriften der Koeniglichen Maiestat zu Franckreich an die Chur und Fuersten Stende und Stett des Heiligen Roemischen Reichs Teutscher Nation. n.p., 1552.

Sibutus, G., *Ad Ferdinandum Hungariae et Bohemiae regem panegyricus. Exhortatio in Turcum.* Wien, 1528.

Suleiman I, *Sulaiman des Gesetzgebers (Kanuni) Tagebuch auf seinem Feldzuge nach Wien im Jahre 935/6 D.H. = J. 1529 N.Chr.* ed. W. F. A. Bernhauer. Wien, 1858.

Treffentlicher und Hochnützlicher Anschlag. n.p., 1541.

Türcken belegerung des Stat Wien MDXXIX. Nürnberg, n.d.

Türckenbiechlin. n.p., 1522(?).

Ulrichi Hutteni Equitis Germani Opera quae reperiri poterunt omnia. E. Böcking, ed. 7 v. Leipzig, 1859–1870.

Verzeichnuss auss was ursachen der künfftig Reichstag auff Egidij nechts fürnemlich aussgeschrieben. n.p., 1522(?).

Viennae Austriae urbis nobilissimae a Sultano Suleymano immanissimo Turcarum tyranno immenso cum exercitu obsessas historia. Augsburg, 1530.

Vives, J. L., *De concordia & discordia in humano genere.* Lugduni, 1532.

────── *Wie der Türck die Christen haltet so under im leben.* tr. C. Nedion, Strassburg, 1532.

Vo einem Scharmützel darinn ein merkliche anzal der Türcken durch hilff des Almechtigen gefangen und erschlagen. n.p., 1532.

Von der schlacht geschehen dem Turcken von dem grossen Sophi in Calimania. Nüremberg, 1514.

Warhafftige und gewise Newe zeytung Wie die Roem. Key. Mey. auff den XX Octobris dess XLI Jahrs mit einer treffentlichen Armada die Statt Algiero zu Erobern. n.p., n.d.

Wahrhaftige anzaygung der geschicht dess Türckischen kriegs. n.p., 1532(?).

Warhaftige newe zeittung von dem Türcke. n.p., 1532.

Warhafftige zeytung das der Grossmeister von Rodis durch seiner Capitanio Saluiaten un Kayserlicher Mauestat Haubtman Andrea Dorea die Stat Modona so der Tuerck vergangner jar mit verlierung etwa vil Tausend man erobert. n.p., 1531.

Was Kaiserlicher Maiestat oberster Haubtman Andrea Dorea Auff dem Meer für Stet dem Türcken nit weyt von Constantinopel abgedrungen und erobert hat. n.p., 1532.

Wie der turkish kaiser sich hat gelegert für Rodyss unnd mit grosser macht und gewaltgestürmet. n.p., 1522.

von Zwickau, J. G., *Vermanung an gantze Deutsche Nation widder den Türckischen Tyrannen.* Wittemberg, 1541.

III. SECONDARY SOURCES

A. General Histories

Brandi, K., *Deutsche Geschichte im Zeitalter der Reformation und Gegenreformation.* 3rd ed. Leipzig, 1942. (The best one-volume study of the German Reformation and Counter-Reformation.)

Browne, E. G., *A Literary History of Persia.* 4 v. London, 1902–1930. (Volume IV contains an outline of Persian history since 1500.)

von Bucholtz, F. B., *Geschichte der Regierung Ferdinand des Ersten.* 9 v. Wien, 1831–38. (Primarily a history of Germany from 1520 to 1560.)

Doeberl, W., *Entwicklungsgeschichte Bayerns.* 3 v. 2nd ed. München, 1908–1931. (Volume I ends with 1648.)

Fueter, E., *Geschichte des Europäischen Staatensystems von 1492–1559.* München, 1919.

von Hammer, J., *Histoire de l'Empire Ottoman.* Tr. J. J. Hellert, 18 v. Paris,

1836–1843. (The most exhaustive history of the Ottoman Empire. Volumes I–VI cover the period through 1574.)

Henderson, E. F., *A Short History of Germany*. 2 v. 2nd ed. New York, 1917.

Histoire de la France depuis les origines jusqu'à la Revolution. ed. E. Lavisse, 9 v. Paris, 1900–1911. (Volumes IV, part 2, and V by C. Petit-Dutaillis and H. Lemonnier cover the period 1422–1559.)

Huber, A., *Geschichte Österreichs*. 6 v. Gotha, 1888–1921. (The fullest and most authoritative history of Austria. Volumes III and IV cover the period from 1437 to the beginning of the seventeenth century.)

Janssen, J., *History of the German People at the Close of the Middle Ages*. Tr. A. M. Christie and M. A. Mitchell, 17 v. London, 1896–1925. (Invaluable for the history of the German Reformation but must be used with caution in view of the author's strong pro-Catholic prejudice.)

Jorga, N., *Geschichte des Osmanischen Reiches*. 5 v. Gotha, 1908–1913. (The most recent of the standard histories of the Ottoman Empire but, in some ways, the least satisfactory. Good on Balkan history but superficial on the main problems of Turkish history.)

Kaser, K., *Deutsche Geschichte zur Zeit Maximilians I*. Stuttgart, 1912. (An excellent study.)

Kosary, D. G., *A History of Hungary*. Cleveland, 1941. (A mediocre textbook.)

von Kraus, V., *Deutsche Geschichte zur Zeit Albrechts II und Friedrichs III. 1438–1486*. Stuttgart, 1905. (An excellent study.)

Krymskii, A. E., *Istoria Turechinii*. 2 v. Kiev, 1924–27. (A good brief survey of Turkish history.)

Lortz, J., *Die Reformation in Deutschland*. 2 v. 3rd ed. Freiburg, 1949.

Mayer, F. M., *Geschichte Österreichs*. 2 v. 3rd ed. Wien, 1909.

von Pastor, L., *Geschichte der Päpste seit dem Ausgang des Mittelalters*. 16 v. Freiburg im Breisgau, 1886–1933.

von Ranke, L., *Deutsche Geschichte im Zeitalter der Reformation*. 5 v. München, 1924.

——— *History of the Reformation in Germany*. Tr. S. Austin, 3 v. London, 1845–47. (Only volumes I–III, covering the period through 1535, have been translated.)

Zarek, O., *The History of Hungary*. London, 1939. (A competent survey.)

Zinkeisen, J. W., *Geschichte des Osmanischen Reiches in Europa*. 7 v. Gotha, 1840–1863. (Exceptionally valuable for the diplomatic relations between the Porte and Western Europe.)

B. Monographs

Bauer, W., *Die Anfänge Ferdinands I*. Wien, 1907. (An excellent study, particularly valuable for the period 1519–1525.)

Baumgarten, H., *Karl V und die deutsche Reformation*. Halle, 1889. (An excellent general survey.)

Bonwetsch, G., *Geschichte des Passauischen Vertrages von 1552.* Göttingen, 1907.

de Boor, A., *Beiträge zur Geschichte des Speirer Reichstages vom Jahre 1544.* Strassburg, 1878.

Brandenburg, E., *Moritz von Sachsen.* Leipzig, 1898.

Brandi, K., *The Emperor Charles V.* Tr. C. W. Wedgwood. New York, 1939. (An impressive biography of Charles V, indispensable for the study of the Emperor's imperial policy.)

—— *Kaiser Karl V.* 2 v. München, 1937–1941.

Brieger, T., *Des Speierer Reichstag von 1526 und die religiöse Frage der Zeit.* Leipzig, 1909.

Diedrichs, P., *Kaiser Maximilian I als politischer Publizist.* Heidelberg, 1932.

Djuvara, T. G., *Cent projets de partage de la Turquie.* Paris, 1914.

von Druffel, A., *Kaiser Karl V und die Römische Curie 1544–1546.* 4 v. München, 1877–1890.

Ebermann, R., *Die Türkenfurcht.* Halle a.S., 1904. (An insufficient account of German reaction to the Turkish threat in the sixteenth century.)

Everth, E., *Die Öffentlichkeit in der Aussenpolitik von Karl V bis Napoleon.* Jena, 1931. (Very brief on the early period.)

Fischer, G., *Die persönliche Stellung und politische Lage König Ferdinands I vor und während der Passauer Verhandlungen des Jahres 1552.* Königsberg, 1891.

Förstemann, K. E., *Urkundenbuch zu der Geschichte des Reichstages zu Augsburg im Jahre 1530.* 2 v. Halle, 1833–35.

Fraknói, W., *Ungarn vor der Schlacht Mohacs, 1524–1526.* Tr. J. H. Schwicker. Budapest, 1886.

——*Matthias Corvinus, König von Ungarn, 1458–1490.* Freiburg im Breisgau, 1891.

Franz, G., *Der deutsche Bauernkrieg.* 2 v. München, 1933–35.

Friedensburg, W., *Der Reichstag zu Speier 1526 in Zusammenhang der politischen und kirchlichen Entwicklung Deutschlands im Reformationszeitalter.* Berlin, 1887. (An excellent study.)

—— *Kaiser Karl V und Papst Paul III (1534–1549).* Leipzig, 1932.

Gerstenberg, L., *Zur Geschichte des deutschen Türkenschauspiels.* Meppen, 1902. (A brief but competent study.)

Gothein, E., *Reformation und Gegen-Reformation.* München, 1924.

de la Gravière, J., *Les Corsaires Barbaresques et la Marine de Soliman le Grand.* Paris, 1887.

von Hammer, J., *Wiens erste aufgehobene tuerkische Belagerung.* Pest, 1829.

Hartung, F., *Karl V und die deutschen Reichstände von 1546 bis 1555.* Halle a.S., 1910.

Hasenclever, A., *Die Politik der Schmalkaldener vor den Ausbruch des Schmalkaldischen Krieges.* Berlin, 1901.

Heidrich, P., *Karl V und die deutschen Protestanten am Vorabend des Schmalkaldischen Krieges*. 2 v. Frankfurt a.M., 1911–12. (Of great value for the study of the period 1541–46.)

Hofmann, K., *Die Konzilsfrage auf den deutschen Reichstagen von 1521–1524*. Mannheim, 1932.

Holborn, H., *Ulrich von Hutten and the German Reformation*. New Haven, 1937.

Jenkins, H. D., *Ibrahim Pasha*. New York, 1911.

Jörg, J. E., *Deutschland in der Revolutions-Periode von 1522 bis 1526*. Freiburg im Breisgau, 1851.

Kalkoff, P., *Die Kaiserwahl Friedrichs IV und Karls V*. Weimar, 1925.

Kamil, B., *Die Türken in der deutschen Literatur bis zum Barock und die Sultansgestalten in den Türkendramen Lowensteins*. Kiel, 1935. (Superficial.)

Kohler, M., *Melanchton und der Islam*. Leipzig, 1938.

Korte, A., *Die Konzilspolitik Karl V in den Jahren 1538–1543*. Halle a.d.S., 1905.

Kühn, J., *Die Geschichte des Speyrer Reichstags 1529*. Leipzig, 1929.

Kühns, W., *Geschichte des Passauischen Vertrages 1552*. Göttingen, 1906.

Kupelwieser, L., *Die Kämpfe Oesterreichs mit den Osmanen vom Jahre 1526 bis 1537*. Wien, 1899.

———*Die Kämpfe Ungarns mit den Osmanen bis zur Schlacht bei Mohács, 1526*. Wien, 1899.

Lamparter, H., *Luthers Stellung zum Türkenkrieg*. München, 1940.

Lane-Poole, S., *The Barbary Corsairs*. New York, 1902.

von Langenn, F. A., *Moritz, Herzog und Churfürst zu Sachsen*. 2 v. Leipzig, 1841.

Lefaivre, A., *Les Magyars pendant la domination ottomane en Hongrie (1526–1722)*. 2 v. Paris, 1902.

Loserth, J., *Innerösterreich und die militärischen Massnahmen gegen die Türken im 16. Jahrhundert*. Graz, 1934.

Maurenbrecher, W., *Karl V und die deutschen Protestanten 1545–1555*. Düsseldorf, 1865. (Valuable despite its age).

Mentz, G., *Johann Friedrich der Grossmütige*. 3 v. Jena, 1903–08. (A distinguished study.)

Merriman, R. B., *Suleiman the Magnificent, 1520–1566*. Cambridge, 1944.

Mignet, M., *Rivalité de François Ier et de Charles-Quint*. 2 v. Paris, 1875. (The best treatment of the subject although somewhat out of date.)

Morel-Fatio, A., *Historiographie de Charles-Quint*. Paris, 1913.

Nykl, A. R., *Discurso sobre la Poesia Castellana*. Baltimore, 1948. (Concerns itself with the history and writings of B. Gjorjevic.)

Pfeffermann, H., *Die Zusammenarbeit der Renaissancepäpste mit den Türken*. Winterthur, 1946. (The most complete, yet superficial, treatment of the subject.)

Philippson, M., *La Contre-Revolution Religieuse au XVIe Siècle*. Brussels, 1884. (Strong anti-Catholic bias.)

Popescu, M., *Die Stellung des Papstthums und des christlichen Abendlandes gegenüber der Türkengefahr von Jahre 1523 bis zur Schlacht bei Mohacs (1526)*. Bucureşti, 1887. (Brief and superficial.)

von Ranke, L., *The Ottoman and the Spanish Empires in the Sixteenth and the Seventeenth Centuries*. London, 1843.

Rassow, P., *Die Kaiser-Idee Karls V*. Berlin, 1932. (An interesting study of Charles' activities in the thirties.)

Richter, A., *Der Reichstag zu Nürnberg, 1524*. Leipzig, 1888.

Roesler, R., *Die Kaiserwahl Karls V*. Wien, 1868.

Rosenberg, W., *Der Kaiser und die Protestanten in den Jahren 1537–1539*. Halle a.S., 1903. (A highly competent study.)

Rosnak, M., *Die Belagerung der Koenigl-Freystadt Guens im Jahre 1532*. Wien, 1789.

Salamon, F., *Ungarn im Zeitalter der Türkenherrschaft*. Tr. G. Jurany. Leipzig, 1887. (An admirable study of Hungarian social, economic, and cultural conditions during the period of Turkish occupation.)

Scholtze, A., *Die Orientalische Frage in der öffentlichen Meinung des sechszehnten Jahrhunderts*. Frankenberg, 1880. (Brief and superficial.)

Schottenloher, K., *Flugblatt und Zeitung*. Berlin, 1922.

Seton-Watson, R. W., *Maximilian I*. Westminster, 1902. (A good brief biography of Maximilian I.)

Springer, J., *Beiträge zur Geschichte des Wormser Reichstages 1544 und 1545*. Leipzig, 1882.

Traut, H., *Kurfürst Joachim II von Brandenburg und der Türkenfeldzug vom Jahre 1542*. Gummersbach, 1892.

Turba, G., *Geschichte des Thronfolgerechts in allen habsburgischen Ländern bis zur pragmatischen Sanktion Kaiser Karls VI*. Wien, 1903.

Ulmann, H., *Kaiser Maximilian I*. 2 v. Stuttgart, 1884–1891. (The best biography of Maximilian I.)

Ursu, J., *Die Auswärtige Politik des Peter Rareş, Fürst von Moldau (1527–1538)*. Wien, 1908.

—— *La Politique Orientale de François I. (1515–1547)*. Paris, 1908. (The best study on the subject.)

Vetter, P., *Die Religionsverhandlungen auf dem Reichstage zu Regensburg 1541*. Jena, 1889.

Waas, G. E., *The Legendary Character of Kaiser Maximilian*. New York, 1941.

Westermann, A., *Die Türkenhilfe und die politisch-kirchlichen Parteien auf dem Reichstag zu Regensburg 1532*. Heidelberg, 1910. (A chronological summary of the negotiations of the Diet of Regensburg.)

Winckelmann, O., *Der Schmalkaldische Bund 1530–1532 und der Nürnberger*

Religionsfriede. Strassburg, 1892. (An excellent study, most valuable for the early history of the Schmalkaldian League.)

Wolf, G., *Der Augsburger Religionsfriede.* Stuttgart, 1890.

C. Articles

Baron, H., "Imperial Reform and the Hapsburgs, 1486–1504," *The American Historical Review,* XLIV (1938–39), 293–303.

Brandi, K., "Passauer Vertrag und Augsburger Religionsfriede," *Historische Zeitschrift,* XCV (1905), 206–264.

Buchanan, H., "Luther and the Turks 1519–1529," *Archiv für Reformationsgeschichte,* 47 (1956), 145–160.

Cosack, C. J., "Zur Literatur der Türkengebete im 16. und 17. Jahrhundert," *Zur Geschichte der evangelischen ascetischen Literatur in Deutschland* (Basel, 1871), 163–242.

Dopsch, A., "Die Weltstaatpolitik der Habsburger im Werden ihres Grossreiches (1477–1526)," *Gesamtdeutsche Vergangenheit. Festgabe für Heinrich Ritter von Srbik zum 60. Geburstag am 10. November 1938* (München, 1938), 55–62.

Engelhardt, A., "Der Nürnberger Religionsfriede von 1532," *Mitteilungen des Vereins für Geschichte der Stadt Nürnberg,* XXXI (Nürnberg, 1933), 17–123. (Indispensable for the study of the Religious Peace of Nürnberg.)

Ennen, Dr., "Der Reichsvicekanzler Dr. Mathias Held," *Annalen des historischen Vereins für den Niederrhein,* XXV (1873), 131–172.

Fiedler, J., "Die Allianz zwischen Kaiser Maximilian I und Vasilji Ivanovic, Grossfürsten von Russland, von dem Jahre 1514," *Sitzungsberichte der philosophisch-historischen Classe der Kaiserlichen Akademie der Wissenschaften,* XLIII (Wien, 1863), 183–289.

Fischer, G., "Ferdinand I und Karl V im Jahre 1552," *Jahrbücher der Königlichen Akademie Gemeinnütziger Wissenschaften zu Erfurt.* Neue Folge, XXXII (Erfurt, 1906), 179–203.

Fischer-Galati, S. A., "Ottoman Imperialism and the Lutheran Struggle for Recognition in Germany, 1520–1529," *Church History,* XXIII (1954), 46–67.

———— "Ottoman Imperialism and the Religious Peace of Nürnberg," *Archiv für Reformationsgeschichte,* 47 (1956), 160–180.

———— "The Turkish Question and the Religious Peace of Augsburg," *Südost-Forschungen,* XV (1956), 290–311.

Forell, G. W., "Luther and the War Against the Turks," *Church History,* XIV (1945), 256–271.

Fuchtel, P., "Der Frankfurter Anstand vom Jahre 1539," *Archiv für Reformationsgeschichte,* 28 (1931), 145–206. (An excellent study.)

Gilliodts van Severen, L., "La Croisade de 1530 ordonnée par Charles-Quint,"

Bibliography 135

Compte Rendu des Séances de la Commission Royale d'Histoire, XVI (Brussels, 1889), 261–282.

Heide, G., "Die Verhandlungen des kaiserlichen Vizekanzlers Held mit den deutschen Ständen (1537–38)," Historisch-politische Blätter für das katolische Deutschland, CII (1888), 713–738.

—— "Nürnberg und die Mission des Vizekanzlers Held," Mitteilungen des Vereins für Geschichte der Stadt Nürnberg, VIII (Nürnberg, 1889), 161–200.

Huber, A., "Die Verhandlungen Ferdinands I mit Isabella von Siebenbürgen 1551–1555," Archiv für österreichische Geschichte, LXXVIII (1892), 1–39.

Kaser, K., "Die auswärtige Politik Maximilians I," Mitteilungen des Instituts für österreichische Geschichtsforschung, XXVI (1905), 612–626.

Kretschmayr, H., "Ludovico Gritti," Archiv für österreichische Geschichte, LXXXIII (1896), 1–107.

Lazius, F., "Luthers Stellung zur türkischen Weltmacht," Baltische Monatschrift, XXXVIII (1891), 263–280.

Liske, X., "Der Congress zu Wien im Jahre 1515," Forschungen zur deutschen Geschichte, VII (Göttingen, 1867), 463–558. (Best study on Maximilian's Hungarian policy.)

Mayer, E. W., "Forschungen zur Politik Karls V während des Augsburger Reichstages von 1530," Archiv für Reformationsgeschichte, 13 (1916), 40–73, 124–146.

Müller, N., "Zur Geschichte des Reichstages zu Regensburg 1541," Jahrbuch für Brandenburgische Kirchengeschichte, IV (1907), 175–248.

Roth, F., "Zur Geschichte des Reichstages zu Regensburg im Jahre 1541," Archiv für Reformationsgeschichte, 2 (1904–05), 250–307; 3 (1905–06), 18–64.

Smolka, S., "Ferdinand des Ersten Bemühungen um die Krone von Ungarn," Archiv für österreichische Geschichte, LVII (1879), 1–172.

von Walter, J., "Bekenntniss und Religionskrieg: zur Geschichte des Augsburger Reichstags 1530," Zeitwende, VI (1930), 339–351.

—— "Der Reichstag zu Augsburg," Luther-Jahrbuch 1930 (München, 1930), 1–90.

Winckelmann, O., "Über die Bedeutung der Vertrage von Kadan und Wien (1534–1535) für die deutschen Protestanten," Zeitschrift für Kirchengeschichte, XI (1890), 212–252.

Wolf, G., "Der Augsburger Interim," Deutsche Zeitschrift für Geschichtswissenschaft. Neue Folge, II (Leipzig, 1897–98), 39–88.

—— "Der Passauer Vertrag und seine Bedeutung für die nächst-folgende Zeit," Neues Archiv für sächsische Geschichte und Altertumskunde, XV (Dresden, 1894), 237–282.

Wolkan, R., "Zu den Türkenliedern des XVI. Jahrhunderts," Festschrift zum VIII. allgemeinen deutschen Neuphilologentage in Wien 1898 (Wien, 1898), 65–77.

Index

Adrian VI, 13–15
Albert Alcibiades of Brandenburg-
  Culmbach, 99, 105, 107–108
Algiers, 59, 85–86
Anna of Hungary, 8, 12
Augsburg: Diet of 1500, 7; Diet of
  1530, 42–49, 51–53, 55, 78, 82,
  86, 112, 114; Confession of, 43,
  46, 50, Diet of 1548, 99; Interim,
  99–100, 102–106, 110, 113; Diet of
  1554–1555, 109, 111, 115; Religious
  Peace of, 109 110, 117
Austria, 4, 6, 12

Balkan Peninsula: wars with Turks,
  1–3, 13–14, 19, 66, 71. *See also*
  Belgrade; Moldavia; Serbia
Barbarossa, Khaireddin, 59–61, 68,
  74, 93
Belgrade, 13–14, 19
Bohemia, 4–6, 8, 10–11
Brunswick, 86–88, 90–92, 95
Buda, 76, 84, 89, 103
Burgundy, 3–5, 11

Cadan, Compact of, 59, 61, 95, 114–
  115, 117
Cambrai, Peace of, 35, 61
Carinthia, 1, 4, 9
Carniola, 1, 4, 9
Catholic League, 65, 72, 80, 88–89,
  94
Catholics: relations with Charles
  V, 12, 24–26, 35, 41–46, 49–55,
  75–78, 80–83, 109, 112–117; rela-
  tions with Ferdinand I, 17–21, 25,

27–30, 32–35, 40, 78, 81, 84–85,
  88–90, 109–117; relations with
  Lutherans, 22, 24, 28–30, 33, 43–
  45, 48–49, 51–56, 58–59, 65–66,
  77–83, 85–94, 103–107, 109, 112–
  117. *See also* Catholic League
Charles V: relations with Catholics,
  12, 24–26, 35, 41–46, 49–55, 75–
  78, 80–83, 109, 112–117; relations
  with Lutherans, 12, 24–26, 41–55,
  60–63, 68–69, 73–83, 85, 87–94,
  98–99, 102–109, 112–117; relations
  with the Papacy, 13–16, 24–26, 38,
  40–41, 47–48, 59, 61–64, 68, 74–
  78, 81, 93–94, 98, 112; wars with
  France, 14–16, 26, 35, 61–62, 68,
  88–89, 91–94, 97, 102, 105, 109,
  112–117; wars with Turks, 33–35,
  50, 54–55, 59–61, 68, 71, 74–77,
  85–86, 92–95, 97, 112–113, 116–117
Clement VII, 26, 38, 40–41, 47–48,
  61, 112–113
Cognac, League of, 16, 26
Constantinople, 1, 5, 9, 14, 31–32,
  38, 40–41, 47, 50, 52, 55–58, 61,
  66, 68, 72, 75–77, 79, 81, 84, 92–
  94, 97, 108, 116
Crespy, Peace of, 94, 97

Diets. *See* Augsburg; Nürnberg;
  Regensburg; Speyer; Worms
Doria, Andrea, 59
Egypt, 13, 21–22
Esslingen, 29

Ferdinand I: succession in Hungary,

8, 12, 27–28, 30–33, 36, 38–39, 41, 50, 52, 57–58, 62, 66–67, 72, 76–77, 84–85, 89, 94, 101–103, 108, 111–117; relations with Lutherans, 17–21, 25, 27–30, 32–36, 40, 46, 48–49, 58–59, 70–73, 78, 81, 84–91, 103–107, 109–117; relations with Catholics, 17–21, 25, 27–30, 32–35, 40, 78, 81, 84–85, 88–90, 109–117; wars with Turks, 27, 33–35, 38–39, 41, 50, 54–55, 57–61, 68, 71, 74–77, 85–86, 92–95, 97, 112–113, 116–117

France, 6, 99; wars with Charles V, 14–16, 26, 35, 61–62, 68, 88–89, 91–94, 97, 102, 105, 109, 112–117; relations with Turks, 38, 59–61, 81, 116; relations with Lutherans, 99–103. *See also* Francis I; Henry II; Italian wars

Francis I, 13–15, 38, 41, 48, 59–61, 63, 75–77, 81, 83, 86, 88–89, 91–94, 97, 112–113, 116

Frankfurt, 69, 71, 74–75, 115; *Anstand*, 73–76, 82, 95, 114, 117

Frederick III, 3–7

Germans: attitude toward Turks, 9–10, 17–18, 29–30, 35, 39–40, 81, 117

Germany: peasant revolts, 10, 23, 108; civil war, 86–88, 96–98, 110, 113; Catholics. *See also* Augsburg; Brunswick; Catholics; Frankfurt; Germans; Holy Roman Empire; Lutherans; Nürnberg; Regensburg; Schmalkaldian War; Speyer; Worms; Würtemberg

Gritti, Ludovico, 58, 62, 66

Grosswardein, Treaty of, 66, 72, 76, 84, 101

Güns, 55, 112, 116

Hannart, Joseph, 21

Hapsburgs. *See* Charles V; Ferdinand I; Frederick III; Maximilian I

Held, Mathias, 63–65, 67, 71

Henry II, 99–100, 102, 105, 107, 109

Henry VIII, 13–14

Henry of Brunswick, 88. *See also* Brunswick

Holy League, 68, 74–75

Holy Roman Emperor. *See* Charles V; Frederick III; Maximilian I

Holy Roman Empire, 3, 5–6, 10, 32, 37, 39–40, 45–46, 52, 54, 60, 80–81, 93, 95, 100, 102, 104–106, 108–110, 112, 114, 117

Hungary, 1–6, 14; Turkish wars, 1–3, 14, 24–27, 50, 54–55, 79, 81, 83–84, 89, 91, 93, 103–104, 108, 112–117; relations with Maximilian I, 5–6, 8, 10; succession of Ferdinand I in, 8, 12, 27–28, 30–33, 36, 38–39, 41, 50, 52, 57–58, 62, 66–67, 72, 76–77, 84–85, 89, 94, 101–103, 108, 111–117. *See also* Buda; John Sigismund; Louis of Hungary and Bohemia; Matthias Corvinus; Mohacs; Territory of Ofen; Zàpolya

Ibrahim Pasha, 39

Imperial Chamber. See *Kammergericht*

Interim. *See* Augsburg, Interim

Isabella, 101, 108

Italian wars, 6, 11, 16, 24, 61, 63

Italy, 5–6, 11–12, 16, 40, 76–77, 81, 83, 111–112. *See also* Italian wars

Joachim of Brandenburg, 67–68

John Frederick of Saxony, 22, 24, 28–30, 36–37, 45–46, 78, 98

John Sigismund, 76, 84, 101, 116

Julius III, 100, 102

Kammergericht, 46, 49, 51–54, 56, 58–59, 62, 65, 67, 69–70, 73–74, 80, 82, 85, 88, 90, 95
King of the Romans. *See* Ferdinand I

Ladislas of Hungary and Bohemia, 5–6, 8, 11
Laski, Hieronimus, 76–77
Linz, Conference of, 102
Lochau, Treaty of, 100, 102
Louis of Bavaria, 47–48, 50, 60
Louis of Hungary and Bohemia, 8, 14–15, 19, 25, 27, 32
Lund, Archbishop of, 69–73
Luther, Martin, 10, 19, 22, 111; attitude toward Turks, 18, 34
Lutherans: relations with Charles V, 12, 24–26, 41–55, 60–63, 68–69, 73–83, 85, 87–94, 98–99, 102–109, 112–117; relations with Ferdinand I, 17–21, 25, 27–30, 32–36, 40, 46, 48–49, 58–59, 70–73, 78, 81, 84 91, 103–107, 109–117; relations with Catholics, 22, 24, 28–30, 33, 43–45, 48 49, 51–56, 58–59, 65–66, 77–83, 85–94, 103–107, 109, 112–117; relations with France, 99–103

Mantua, Council of, 63–64, 68, 74–75
Mary of Burgundy, 3, 5
Mary of Hapsburg, 8
Matthias Corvinus, 3–5
Maurice of Saxony, 100, 102–104
Maximilian I: dynastic policy, 5, 8, 11–12; foreign policy, 5–11; relations with Hungary, 5–6, 8, 10; German policy, 6–10; relations with the Turks, 8–10
Mediterranean, 5, 13, 59–61, 68, 71, 74, 76–77, 92–93, 95, 97, 113, 116
Mohacs, 12, 16, 18, 27, 29

Moldavia, 1, 66, 71

Naves, Count of, 82, 86
Nice, 62, 68
Nürnberg, 22, 51, 58, 70; Diet of 1522, 20; Diet of 1524, 21–24; Diet of 1532, 52–54, 56; Religious Peace of, 54–56, 58–59, 61–70, 73, 75, 82, 87, 94–95, 112, 114, 117; Diet of 1543–1544, 89–91, 95

Ofen, 50, 52. *See also* Territory of Ofen
Ottoman Empire. *See* Constantinople; Suleiman I the Magnificent; Turks

Papacy, 6, 14, 16, 59, 68; relations with Charles V, 13–16, 24–26, 38, 40–41, 47–48, 59, 61–64, 68, 74–78, 81, 93–94, 98, 112. *See also* Adrian VI; Clement VII; Julius III; Paul III
Passau: Conference of, 103–104; Treaty of, 105–110, 115, 117
Paul III, 61–63, 74–78, 81, 93–94, 98
Peasant revolts, Germany, 10, 23, 108
Persia, 13, 57, 60. *See also* Thamasp
Peter Rareş, 66, 71
Philip of Hesse, 22, 28–30, 36–37, 58–60, 95, 98
Philip of Spain, 101, 110
Porte. *See* Constantinople
Pressburg, Treaty of, 4, 6
Protestants. *See* Lutherans

Regensburg: Diet of 1527–1528, 30–31; Diet of 1532, 49, 51–55; Diet of 1541, 78–79, 81, 83–85, 90–91, 94–95, 115; Book of, 82–83; Declaration of, 82–83, 117
Rhodes, 13–15

Schmalkalden, League of, 46, 58,

64, 66, 88–89, 93–94, 98. *See also* Lutherans
Schmalkaldian War, 86–88, 96–98, 110, 113
Schmalkaldians. *See* Lutherans; Schmalkalden, League of
Schweinfurt, 52
Serbia, 1–2
Sforza, Bianca, 8, 11
Spain, 6, 8, 10–11, 101
Speyer: 22, 35, 48; Diet of 1526, 23, 25–31, 33–34, 36, 115, 117; Diet of 1529, 32–37, 40, 44, 112; Protestation of, 35, 37; Diet of 1542, 83–92, 94–95, 117; Diet of 1544, 92, 94–95
Staathalter. See Ferdinand I
Strassburg, 22
Styria, 1, 4, 9, 55
Suleiman I the Magnificent, 11, 13, 19, 24, 38, 55, 57–58, 60–62, 66, 76–77, 81, 84, 89, 92–94, 97–98, 102, 108, 115

Territory of Ofen, 84–85, 89, 108, 115
Thamasp, 57–58, 61, 94, 97, 108
Trent, Council of, 94, 98–100, 102, 104, 114
Tunis, 60–61
Turks: wars in Balkan Peninsula, 1–3, 13–14, 19, 66, 71; wars in Hungary, 1–3, 14, 24–27, 50, 54–55, 79, 81, 83–84, 89, 91, 93, 103–104, 108, 112–117; relations with

Maximilian I, 8–10; attitude of Germans toward, 9–10, 17–18, 29–30, 35, 39–40, 81, 117; attitude of Luther toward, 18, 34; wars with Charles V, 33–35, 50, 54–55, 59–61, 68, 71, 74–77, 85–86, 92–95, 97, 112–113, 116–117; wars with Ferdinand I, 27, 33–35, 38–39, 41, 50, 54–55, 57–61, 68, 71, 74–77, 85–86, 92–95, 97, 112–113, 116–117; relations with France, 38, 59–61, 81, 116. *See also* Constantinople; Suleiman I the Magnificent

Ulm, 22
Ulrich of Würtemberg, 58–59. *See also* Würtemberg

Venice, 3, 5–6, 9, 13, 68, 76
Vienna, 4, 20, 38–39, 41, 55, 85, 88; Treaty of 1515, 8, 27; Siege of, 35–36, 38, 116

Weissenburg, Agreement of, 101–103, 108
William of Bavaria, 47–48, 50, 60
Worms: Diet of 1495, 7; Diet of 1521, 19; Edict of, 24–25, 111, 114; *Türkentag,* 70, 74; theological discussions, 77–78
Würtemberg, 58–59, 95, 115

Zápolya, John, 8, 27–28, 30–33, 36, 48, 50, 57–58, 62, 66–67, 76, 84, 108, 115–116

21011

DB
65.3
F5
1972

Fischer-Galati,
Stephen A.
    Ottoman imperial-
ism and German
protestantism,
1521-1555

DATE DUE
